Chile

Chile

BY MICHAEL BURGAN

Enchantment of the World™
Second Series

Children's Press®

An Imprint of Scholastic Inc.

NEW YORK   TORONTO   LONDON   AUCKLAND   SYDNEY
MEXICO CITY   NEW DELHI   HONG KONG
DANBURY, CONNECTICUT

Frontispiece: Waterfall in Torres del Paine National Park, Patagonia

Consultant: Richard Abisla, International Observer, Civic Council of Grassroots and
        Indigenous Groups of Honduras

Please note: All statistics are as up-to-date as possible at the time of publication.

Book production by Herman Adler

Library of Congress Cataloging-in-Publication Data

Burgan, Michael.
  Chile / by Michael Burgan.
      p. cm. — (Enchantment of the world. Second series)
  Includes bibliographical references and index.
  ISBN-13: 978-0-531-20650-8
  ISBN-10: 0-531-20650-5
  1. Chile—Juvenile literature. I. Title. II. Series.
  F3058.5.B87 2009
  983—dc22   2008044175

1 2 3 4 5 6 7 8 9 10 R 19 18 17 16 15 14 13 12 11 10   62

Chile

Cover photo:
Chilean boy
on a horse

Contents

Vicuñas

Chilean child

A Land of Contrasts

THE NORTH OF CHILE RUNS LIKE A RIBBON ALONG THE southwestern coast of South America. There you will find some of the driest desert on Earth. But unlike many deserts, this one is not scorching hot. Instead, the temperature is usually comfortable, and in winter, it sometimes dips below freezing. In the south of Chile are damp, rainy forests. And at the far southern tip of Chile, huge mountains of ice called glaciers tower overhead. In some spots in Chile, you can look to the west and see the Pacific Ocean while the mammoth Andes Mountains cast a shadow not far behind you.

Opposite: **These giant candelabra cactuses are among the few plants that grow in the deserts of northern Chile.**

O'Higgins Glacier flows into a lake in Bernardo O'Higgins National Park in southern Chile.

Chile is a nation of contrasts, of dry and wet, warm and cold, high and low. But the contrasts go beyond its geography. Santiago, the capital, bustles with activity. More than 6 million people live there, working in government, education, and businesses of all kinds. Hundreds of miles to the south, some Chileans have a completely different life. In the forested region of Araucanía, many Mapuche people live as their ancestors did hundreds of years ago. Women spin yarn and weave by hand, and people bring goods to market in horse-drawn carts.

Santiago is a thriving, energetic city. It is Chile's financial and cultural heart.

CHILE

- Cities of more than 200,000 people
- ○ Other cities
- ✪ National capital
- ∴ Archaeological site

0   400 miles

0   400 kilometers

PERU

BOLIVIA

BRAZIL

PARAGUAY

BRAZIL

ARGENTINA

URUGUAY

Lauca Nat'l Park

Arica

Iquique

Calama

Loa R.

Los Flamencos Nat'l Reserve

Antofagasta

Diego de Almagro

Copiapó

Humboldt Penguin Nat'l Reserve

Vallenar

La Serena

Coquimbo

Ovalle

Fray Jorge Nat'l Park

Illapel

La Calera

Viña del Mar

Santiago

Valparaíso

El Morado Nat'l Mon

San Bernardo

Puente Alto

Rancagua

Constitución

Talca

Maule R.

Chillán

Talcahuano

Concepción

Los Angeles

Cañete

Bío-Bío R.

Temuco

Villarrica

Valdivia

Calle-Calle R.

Osorno

Llanquihue Lake

Monte Verde

Puerto Montt

Chiloé Nat'l Park

Castro

Gulf of Corcovado

Las Guaitecas Nat'l Reserve

Coihaique

Laguna San Rafael Nat'l Park

General Carrera Lake

Baker R.

Bernardo O'Higgins Nat'l Park

Puerto Natales

Strait of Magellan

Torres del Paine Nat'l Park

Punta Arenas

Tierra del Fuego

Hernando de Magallanes Nat'l Park

Alberto de Agostini Nat'l Park

PACIFIC OCEAN

ATLANTIC OCEAN

N
W   E
S

Chile

German Chileans enjoy the scenery of their village in southern Chile. An estimated one million Chileans have German roots.

Spain once ruled Chile, and Spanish settlers brought their language, farm animals, and political systems to the region. Today, most Chilean people still follow Spain's traditional religion, Roman Catholicism. But other immigrants from countries such as Germany, Great Britain, Lebanon, and Syria have come to Chile seeking a new start. They have added to the cultural mix that makes up Chile today.

Over the years, Chileans have also seen changes in how they have been ruled. Under Spanish control, orders came from beyond the country's borders. After winning their independence in the 19th century, Chileans struggled to build a democratic society that protected everyone's rights. At times, Chile came under the control of a single strong ruler. Other times, the people have had a greater say through their elected officials.

One of Chile's darkest periods began in 1973, when the military forced out the elected president and took over the government. For years afterward, the government sometimes tortured or killed Chileans who seemed to pose a threat to the people in power. Those years of terror ended in 1990, and Chile is once again a democratic country.

Chilean citizens gather in a school gymnasium in Santiago to vote in the 2005 presidential election.

Some of the conflicts in Chile's government have dealt with the question of who should control the country's wealth. Natural resources, especially minerals, have long been a source of wealth in Chile. At times, only a small number of people benefited from the sale of these resources. Political parties rose to protect the rights of workers and the poor, trying to give them a greater share of the country's riches. The clash between these parties and others representing the wealthy led to some of the political turmoil the country has faced.

Copper mining is an important part of Chile's economy. Copper accounts for about one-third of Chile's exports.

A family enjoys a walk through the streets of Valparaíso. Family is central to Chilean life.

If Chileans sometimes disagree on political and economic issues, most can agree on some things. Chileans cherish their families and are usually close to relatives. Getting married and having children is an important goal for many people. Chileans tend to like traditional ways of doing things, yet as a nation, they can embrace change. Women traditionally played only a small role in Chile's political and business affairs, but in 2006, the country elected its first woman president.

Chileans are known as hard workers, but they also know how to have fun. They enjoy entertaining guests, and the lucky visitors quickly learn that this diverse land and its people have much to offer.

Desert, Mountains, Ocean, and Ice

C HILE FORMS A LONG, THIN STRIP ALONG THE WESTERN edge of the southern half of South America. Its average width is just 110 miles (177 kilometers), but the country covers a total of 292,260 square miles (756,950 sq km), an area slightly larger than Texas. To Chile's west are 2,650 miles (4,265 km) of Pacific Ocean coastline. The Andes mark the country's eastern edge. These mountains lie along the border with Peru, Chile's northern neighbor, and with Argentina and Bolivia, its neighbors to the east.

Opposite: **Chile's long coastline is a mixture of cliffs, bays, and spectacular beaches.**

The jagged Paine Mountains rise in the Andes of southern Chile.

Chile's Geographic Features

Highest Elevation: Ojos del Salado, 22,572 feet (6,880 m)

Lowest Elevation: Sea level, along the coast

Longest River: Loa, 275 miles (443 km)

Largest Lake: General Carrera (shared with Argentina), 714 square miles (1,850 sq km)

Most Remote Island: Easter Island, about 2,200 miles (3,500 km) west of the mainland

Highest Recorded Temperature: 106°F (41°C), in Los Angeles, February 9, 1944

Lowest Recorded Temperature: −35°F (−37°C), in Coyaique Alto, June 21, 2002

Highest Average Annual Precipitation: about 200 inches (500 cm), at the Strait of Magellan

Lowest Average Annual Precipitation: 0.03 inches (0.08 cm), at Arica

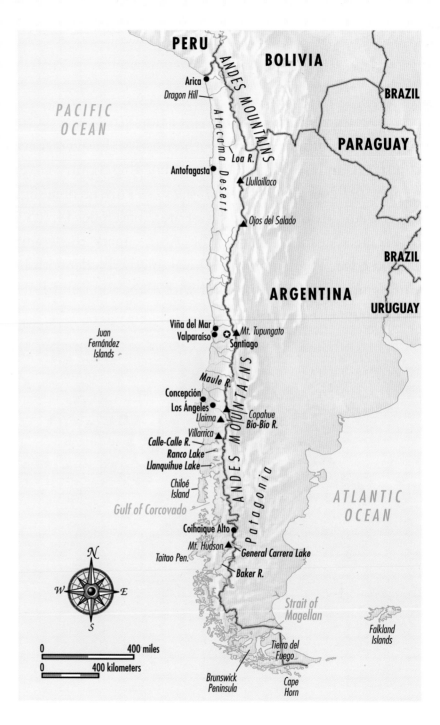

Thousands of islands are also part of Chile. It shares the largest of these, Tierra del Fuego, with Argentina. Other notable islands include the Chiloé group, Easter Island, and the Juan Fernández Islands. Chile also claims a part of Antarctica, as do several other nations. That frozen continent is about 600 miles (950 km) from the tip of southern Chile.

Chile's long, narrow land can be divided into five regions, each with its own landforms and climate. The towering Andes Mountains, the highest mountain range in the Americas, run down the eastern side of all these regions.

Easter Island is located 2,200 miles (3,500 km) from mainland Chile. Long ago, the people of Easter Island carved 887 giant stone figures, called *moai*.

Activity Below the Earth

The Earth's outer layer is made up of large pieces of rock called tectonic plates. The movement of these plates creates volcanoes and earthquakes, and places where plates meet are particularly prone to activity. Several tectonic plates meet near South America's Pacific coast, and Chile has been the site of some of the strongest earthquakes of recent centuries. In 1960, an earthquake with a magnitude of 9.5 hit Valdivia. It was the most powerful earthquake ever recorded. The quake killed hundreds of people and produced a huge tsunami, a tidal wave that wiped out entire villages.

The Northern Regions

The northernmost region is the Norte Grande, the "Great North." This region is the heart of Chile's copper-mining industry. It is also the site of the Atacama Desert, the driest desert in the world. Most people in the Norte Grande live along the Pacific coast, where the land is flat. Not far inland, the land begins to rise into small mountains. This coastal range runs south through much of the country and can reach heights of 7,000 feet (2,100 meters). Farther east in the Norte Grande are hills and flat, elevated land called the *altiplano*, or "high plain." The elevation of the altiplano reaches about 11,000 feet (3,400 m). High in the Andes in the eastern part of the Norte Grande is El Tatio, the largest geyser field in the Southern Hemisphere. A geyser is hot water under the ground that erupts skyward in a burst of steam. El Tatio has more than 80 active geysers.

Chile's longest river flows through the Norte Grande. The Loa River forms a U-shape as it follows its 275-mile (443 km) course from the Andes to the Pacific Ocean.

South of the Norte Grande is the second northern region, the Norte Chico, or "Little North." This region begins south of the city of Antofagasta and ends just north of Santiago. The Norte Chico is not as dry as the Norte Grande. It has valleys where Chileans raise crops and cattle. Melting snow in the Andes feeds small rivers that flow through these valleys. On the northern edge of this region is Chile's highest peak, Ojos del Salado. Reaching a height of 22,572 feet (6,880 m), it is the tallest active volcano in the world.

The massive Ojos del Salado volcano straddles the border between Chile and Argentina.

Farmers grow many different crops in the Valle Central. This almond orchard is located near the city of Rancagua, south of Santiago.

The Valle Central

The Valle Central, or "Central Valley," is the heart of Chile. Most of the nation's residents live in this region, which includes Santiago and other major cities such as Valparaíso and Concepción. The Valle Central contains the country's best farmland, and in the southern part of the valley are hills where Chileans grow trees for lumber and paper.

The Valley of the Moon

In the Atacama Desert lies an eerie landscape called the Valley of the Moon. Over time, wind and water have sculpted pillars in the valley and given the land an extraordinary texture that reminds visitors of the surface of the moon.

Looking at Chile's Cities

The capital city of Santiago and one of its suburbs, Puente Alto, are the two largest cities in Chile. The next-largest city is Antofagasta, which is home to more than 340,000 people. Antofagasta, which lies in the dry north, is in the heart of Chile's copper-mining region. The city's Regional Museum offers information on the Atacama Desert and the history of the area.

Viña del Mar (right), which is Spanish for "Vineyard by the Sea," is the nation's fourth-largest city, with about 300,000 residents. Founded in 1874, it is fringed with white-sand beaches and is a popular tourist spot. The president's summer residence is located in Viña del Mar. Each February, the city is the site of the Viña del Mar International Song Festival, which features a song competition and performances by leading popular musicians. It is one of the most important music festivals in Latin America.

Valparaíso (left), which means "Paradise Valley," is a port city in the Valle Central that is also home to nearly 300,000 people. It has many fine homes built during the 19th century, when the city was a major international seaport. The city has many steep hills. Sharply inclined railways called funiculars carry visitors and residents up the hills. Valparaíso also has a museum dedicated to one of Chile's greatest writers, Pablo Neruda, who lived there during the 1950s.

Concepción, in the south, has a population of about 225,000. Founded in 1550, it has been destroyed several times by earthquakes. Today, the city is home to several major universities and is known for its active cultural life.

South of the Valle Central is the Sur—the "South." Farmers raise grain and cattle in this rainy, humid region. The Sur is sometimes called Chile's Lake District. Major lakes here include Ranco and Llanquihue, the second largest in Chile. An important river in the region, the Bío-Bío, provides water for human use, including irrigation. Valdivia, the major city in the region, sits along the Calle-Calle, one of the few rivers in Chile that can handle large boats.

The Zona Austral, or "Southern Zone," is the southernmost part of Chile. In this region, Chile reaches its narrowest width, just 9 miles (15 km) across. The Zona Austral includes most of

The town of Puerto Varas lies along the coast of Lake Llanquihue. Osorno Volcano looms in the background.

the country's islands along with Patagonia, the southern tip of South America, which Chile shares with Argentina. The region provides Chile's most dramatic natural beauty. In Patagonia, the Andes reach their end, and fjords—narrow waterways that flow between steep cliffs—break up the coastline. Part of Patagonia is covered with glaciers, slow-moving fields of ice. The region also includes the Baker, Chile's widest and swiftest river, and General Carrera, the country's largest lake.

Off the southern tip of Chile is the remote island of Tierra del Fuego—"Land of Fire." The indigenous, or native, people of the island once lit large bonfires along the shore. The Strait of Magellan, a narrow waterway named for the Portuguese explorer Ferdinand Magellan, separates the island from the mainland. South of Tierra del Fuego is Cape Horn, where the Atlantic and the Pacific oceans meet.

The rugged cliffs of Cape Horn mark the southernmost tip of South America.

Many rivers and creeks in Chile are dry part of the year. The mud in this creek bed in northern Chile has dried up and cracked into pieces.

Climate

Chile's diverse regions have widely different climates. Even within one region, mountains and the ocean create small areas with their own distinct local climates. Because Chile is located below the equator, its seasons are opposite those in North America and Europe. Summer is from December to March, and winter runs from June to September.

In some parts of the desert of the Norte Grande, no rain falls for years. But in the higher elevations near Bolivia, it rains during the summer, sometimes creating small lakes. Along the coast of this region, heavy fogs roll in during the early morning hours. The mountains keep the fog trapped near the ocean, and the moisture in the fog helps provide water for plants. Temperatures in the Norte Grande are cool and don't swing widely between summer and winter. At sea level, summer temperatures average 69 degrees Fahrenheit (21° Celsius) and winter temperatures average about 57°F (14°C). The Norte Chico gets more rain, especially in the winter. Its average summer and winter temperatures are slightly lower than those in the Norte Grande.

Fog covers the mountains of Torres del Paine National Park.

In the Valle Central, summers are usually hot and dry and winters are comfortable, if sometimes rainy. Some snow falls close to the mountains, but rarely along the coast. The amount of rain increases as you travel farther south in the region.

Chile's heaviest rains fall in the southern regions, with some areas getting 200 inches (500 centimeters) of precipitation each year. Winters are not usually very cold in the Sur. Valdivia, for example, has an average winter temperature of 46°F (8°C). The southernmost part of Chile has the country's coldest temperatures. Punta Arenas, the major city in the Zona Austral, has an average winter temperature of 37°F (3°C). In general, throughout the country, the coldest and snowiest weather is in the Andes Mountains.

A snowboarder glides down the slopes near Llaima Volcano.

Ice Melts, Problems Grow

Chile's mountain glaciers are an important source of water for crops, animals, and humans. Today, that natural resource is in danger of melting away. Most scientists believe that average temperatures around the world are rising, a situation called global warming. Human activity, including burning oil and coal for energy, have contributed to this change in the climate.

The rising temperatures are melting Chile's Andean glaciers. In southern Chile, one glacier has already melted. The glacier had served as a dam, holding back the waters of a lake. With the glacier gone, the water drained from the lake, and the lake disappeared.

Typically, mountain glaciers that melt in the spring have provided some of Santiago's water. In the past, winter snows and cold temperatures built the glaciers up again. But global warming has stopped this from happening, and in the summer months, more of the glaciers melt. Without the glaciers, Chile and its neighbors could face serious water shortages in the decades to come.

Wonderful
Wildlife

C HILE'S VARYING CLIMATES AND GEOGRAPHIC REGIONS give it a wide range of plant and animal life. Chile helps preserve its plants and animals with more than 80 natural parks and reserves scattered across the country. But even with these special safety zones for wildlife, some Chilean plants and animals are facing extinction.

Opposite: **Wild donkeys live in the Atacama Desert of northern Chile.**

Life in the North

Water is vital to wildlife, and only a few plants and animals have found a way to survive in the dry north of Chile. Some plant seeds remain under the dry ground for years and sprout

Wildflowers bloom in the Chilean desert after a rare rain.

only after a rare rain. Some of these colorful desert flowers include the *suspiro de campo* and the *pata de huanaco*. Cactuses also grow there. Scorpions, lizards, and insects live in the Atacama Desert, but few mammals survive there.

A greater variety of wildlife thrives in the coastal regions and mountains of the Norte Grande. Seals and seabirds, such as pelicans and seagulls, live along the seacoast. In the high plains east of the desert live foxes, a small deer called the taruca, and a rodent called the vizcacha, which is related to the guinea pig. The Andean hairy armadillo is also found there. The mountains are home to the puma, a large member

Humboldt penguins and South American sea lions share the rocky coast of Patagonia. Male South American sea lions can grow 9 feet (2.7 m) long.

of the cat family. In the higher elevations live the chinchilla, another type of rodent. In the 19th century, hunters targeted chinchillas for their incredibly soft fur, and the creatures almost became extinct. Today, they remain rare. The rhea, a large bird related to the ostrich, also lives in this region. Rheas can't fly, but they are fast runners.

Lauca National Park is home to many of the animals found in the altiplano and the mountains, as well as more than 130 species of birds. These include Andean flamingos and various kinds of ducks, condors, and eagles. The park also has some unique plant life, such as the quenoa and the llareta. The quenoa grows at a higher elevation than any other tree in the world. Because of the harsh mountain conditions, the tree remains short and bushy. The llareta is a green, bushy plant that grows very slowly—less than 1 inch (2.5 cm) per year.

Pumas are the second-largest cats found in the Americas. Males stand about 2.5 feet (75 cm) at the shoulder.

The "Camels" of Chile

In the mountains of Chile, several species related to camels, including llamas, have adapted to the high altitude and sometimes harsh climate. People of the Andes domesticated llamas thousands of years ago, using them to carry loads along narrow mountain passes and to provide wool from their hairy coats. Today, people also raise alpacas for their wool.

Two llama relatives live wild in Chile. Vicuña (above) stand about 36 inches (91 cm) at the shoulder. They have the softest wool of the camel relatives. So many were killed for their wool that they were once in danger of extinction. Guanacos grow to about 48 inches (122 cm) at the shoulder. They are speedy runners, reaching up to 40 miles per hour (64 kph).

In the Norte Chico, a little more rain falls, and a greater variety of wildlife can be found. Some drier areas also receive moisture from the ocean fogs that roll in and cling to the shore. In some locations, the moisture helps papaya and cinnamon trees and different kinds of cactus grow. Fray Jorge National Park, near the coast, features a wide variety of wildlife, including otters, foxes, vizcachas, and chinchillas.

The birds of the Norte Chico include ducks, eagles, hummingbirds, and the Chilean mockingbird. Insects, more common here than in the desert region, include beetles, dragonflies, horseflies, and wasps. Some of these bugs provide food for lizards and snakes. Several offshore islands serve as nesting spots for Humboldt penguins, and the nearby waters are home to sea lions and bottle-nosed dolphins. Tuna, sole, and other deepwater fish live all along Chile's coast, from north to south.

Vizcachas live in many parts of Chile. They live in groups and sometimes maintain the same burrow for several generations.

The Valle Central has most of Chile's population, so large parts of its land are developed for human activity. But many forests remain south of Santiago, and the mountains and oceans create welcoming environments for wildlife. Animals of the forest include foxes, rabbits, and a rodent called a coipo, which looks something like a beaver with a long tail. Another rodent, the degu, is the most common mammal in central Chile. A degu looks a little like a large gerbil. If an enemy grabs its tail, the degu spins around until its tail skin tears off. Then it pulls away and escapes. Pampas cats, which are also known as mountain cats, live only in the mountains of central Chile. About the same size as house cats, pampas cats come out at night to hunt birds and small animals.

Pampas cats live high in the mountains of Chile but are rarely found elsewhere.

Island Wildlife

Chile has three major island groups in the Pacific Ocean that are home to some of the country's most diverse wildlife. The closest to the mainland is Chiloé. Its main island is the second largest in South America after Tierra del Fuego. Isla Grande ("Big Island") has its own national park, which features rare animals such as the Chilean shrew opossum.

Farther out in the Pacific, about 400 miles (650 km) west of the coast, are the Juan Fernández Islands. More than 100 kinds of plant and animal life exist only on these remote, rocky islands. The Juan Fernández sea lion (above) and the Juan Fernández firecrown, a hummingbird, are both endangered. Much more plentiful are the cod and lobsters that live in the waters off the islands.

Easter Island is the most remote of Chile's Pacific islands. It is also known as Rapa Nui. Millions of palm trees once covered Easter Island, but few remain today.

No mammals are native to the island—rats and other creatures came with human settlers. Just two types of small lizards and some insects are native to the island. Some tropical birds such as sooty terns (below) come to Easter Island to nest.

A Caring Father

Darwin's frog lives along streams in the Valle Central. It is named for Charles Darwin, an English scientist who searched Chile for wildlife in the 1830s. He later came up with the theory of evolution, which explains that species slowly change over time to ensure their survival. Darwin's frogs have evolved an unusual way to have babies. The female lays her eggs on moist ground, and the eggs slowly become tadpoles. The father frog then scoops the tadpoles into his mouth. They live there for a few weeks, before leaving their father's mouth as fully formed, tiny frogs.

The giant hummingbird grows to about 8 inches (20 cm) long, around twice the length of an average hummingbird.

Birds of the central region include the giant hummingbird—the largest of its kind in the world—and the rare burrowing parrot. These yellow-bellied birds build their nests inside small tunnels found in steep, rocky cliffs. Another parrot, the tricahue, lives high in the Andes of the Valle Central. Near some of the region's lakes you'll spot black-necked swans and other waterbirds. Fish in some of these lakes include a type of mackerel called the *pejerrey chileno*. A reptile found near streams is the Chilean iguana. This endangered species has been compared to an overfed lizard. It reaches about 18 inches (46 cm) in length.

The plant life of the Valle Central includes a group of trees with short, hard, thick leaves that grow in areas with mild winters. Some of these trees include the peumo, a type of laurel tree native to Chile. The Chilean palm tree was once common in the region, but Spanish settlers cut it down for its sweet sap. Today, two areas in Chile have forests set aside for the palm where it cannot be cut down. The Chilean palm is a massive tree, with a trunk width up to 5 feet (1.5 m) in diameter and a height of up to 90 feet (27 m). Some of these trees live to be a thousand years old.

The monkey puzzle tree is native to the Valle Central. It got its name from its sharp, prickly needles that make it difficult to climb.

Nature in the South

The Sur region is also home to unusual wildlife. The Valdivian Coastal Range has a great number of species found only there or in neighboring Argentina, including the giant otter, which can reach 5 feet (1.5 m) long. The southern pudu, the world's smallest deer, lives in thick forests. It grows to be just 18 inches (46 cm) tall.

Almost 60 kinds of birds live along the Sur's coast. One of them is the rock cormorant, which often raises its young on cliffs near the water. The region is also home to the world's largest woodpecker, the Magellanic woodpecker. Trees along the coast include the olivillo and the alerce. Alerces are large trees that are one of the longest-lived species on Earth. Some alerces have been found to be more than 3,600 years old.

Foxes, pumas, guiñas (a type of bobcat), a deer called the huemul, and many other creatures live in the Andes of the Sur. Birds soaring overhead include eagles, Andean condors, and peuquitos, a type of hawk.

The rock cormorant lives along the coast of the Sur region. It feeds mainly on small fish that it snatches from the water.

Symbols of Chile

Chile's national animal is the huemul (above), a deer that lives in Chile's southern mountains. Because it can easily scramble over rocky ground, the huemul sometimes seems more like a mountain goat than a deer. Hunting and the destruction of wild lands have endangered the huemul, and fewer than 2,000 remain in the southern Andes.

Chile's national flower is the copihue (above). It grows on vines in the country's forests from Valparaíso south to Osorno, in the Sur. The copihue is sometimes called the bellflower, because of its shape. The plant produces edible fruit, and its root can be used to make medicine. Cutting and selling wild copihues is against the law.

Wildlife in a Harsh Region

Few people live in the Zona Austral because of its harsh climate, but various kinds of wildlife survive there, including muskrats, pumas, and guanacos. Albatrosses, penguins, and other waterbirds also live in the region.

Ancient Animal Uncovered

Milodón Cave Natural Monument, near Punta Arenas, pays tribute to an ancient giant of Chile. In 1895, a German settler found a piece of animal skin in the cave. Bones were later discovered. An Argentine scientist said they came from the mylodon, or giant sloth. When the animal stood on its rear legs, it was almost twice as tall as an adult human. The mylodon lived in this part of Chile more than 10,000 years ago. But the scientist who studied the skin claimed that the sloth it came from had died recently, and people began to search the area for living mylodons. None were found, and more recent tests showed that the mylodon skin found in 1895 was indeed 10,000 years old. The cave's damp air had helped keep it fresh.

The waters off the Zona Austral, extending down to Antarctica, are filled with wildlife of all sizes. It ranges from krill, which look like tiny shrimp, to the giant blue whales that eat krill by the ton every day. Squid and octopuses live in the chilly waters of southern Chile. Closer to shore live seals and sea lions.

The blue whale is the largest animal on Earth, with some growing more than 100 feet (30 m) long. Blue whales were hunted to near extinction in the 20th century and remain endangered.

Humans and the Environment

Human activity has threatened the survival of some plants and animals in Chile. Loggers cut down trees, both reducing the tree population and destroying the habitat for animals. At times, the disappearance of one animal can affect another. The number of Andean cats has fallen because humans hunt chinchillas and other animals the cats feed on.

Chile has created a system of 47 national reserves, which are designed to protect wildlife that might face extinction. Humboldt Penguin National Reserve spans three islands in the Norte Chico. It is intended to protect the Humboldt penguin, the most endangered penguin species in the world.

The Humboldt penguin is found only along the Pacific coast of Peru and Chile.

Problems from Abroad

Beavers native to North America now live in the Zona Austral, and they are creating problems. Years ago, trappers brought beavers to Chile to raise them for their prized fur. But the business idea did not work, and the beaver population grew wildly. Today, 50,000 beavers are gnawing their way through forests in southern Patagonia. In 2003, the Chilean government started a program to trap the beavers, hoping to save local forests and prevent the beavers from migrating farther north.

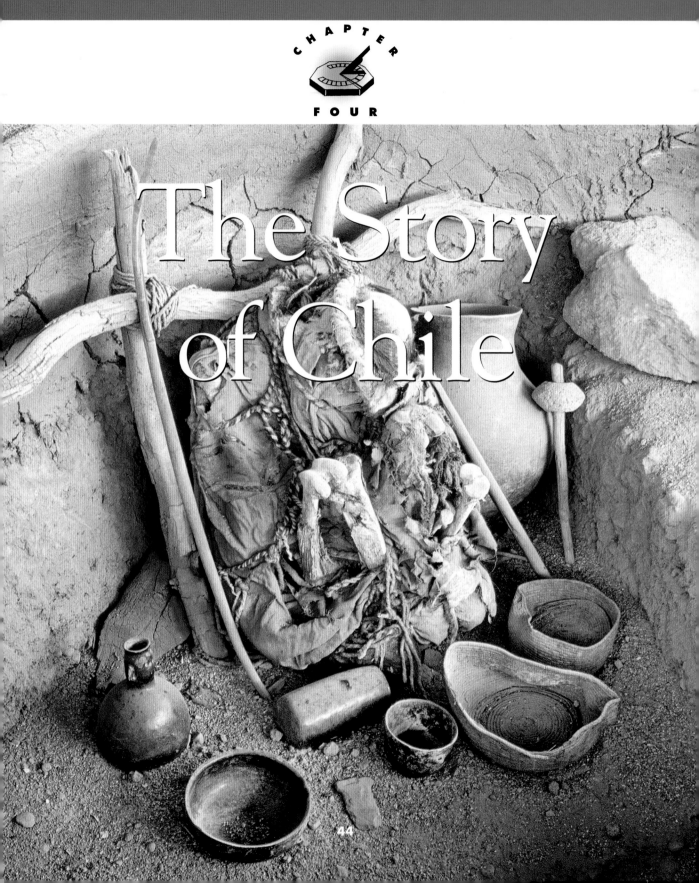

The Story of Chile

A T LEAST 14,000 YEARS AGO, PEOPLE FROM ASIA crossed to the Americas and reached the southern region of Chile. They first settled in a spot now called Monte Verde.

The first Chileans slowly moved out from their spot in Monte Verde. Some stayed along the coast, relying on the sea for food. They collected shellfish and ate seaweed. Other settlers moved inland, near rivers. They hunted for food, sometimes killing mastodons, ancient relatives of the elephant. The inland settlers also gathered wild fruit, and some learned to herd llamas. They were nomads, moving from spot to spot to find food.

One group of early settlers, the Chinchorro, settled in northern Chile around 6000 BCE. The Chinchorro were among the first people in history to turn dead people into mummies. To make a mummy, they removed the skin, took the flesh off the bones, and then assembled the bones back into a skeleton. They placed clay and plants around the bones to represent muscles and organs, put the skin back on the body, and covered it with an ash paste. The dry desert air helped preserve the mummies, which are still occasionally found in northern Chile.

Opposite: **Archaeological sites such as this ancient burial pit reveal much about the early inhabitants of Chile.**

The Chinchorro people used wigs and clay masks when creating mummies such as this one.

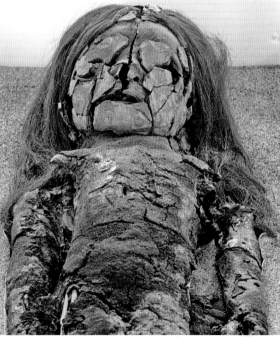

Settlers who moved into northern Chile eventually came into contact with Peruvian farmers who had learned how to raise crops. The Chileans learned to farm and began to build villages around their fields. They raised potatoes, corn, beans, and peppers. By 1000 CE, the indigenous peoples of Chile were farming over a wide area, while still hunting, fishing, and gathering food as well. They made clothing and blankets from llama wool. Early Spanish settlers called the main indigenous group in central and southern Chile the Araucanos. Today they are called the Mapuche.

Desert Giant

About a thousand years ago, people in the north of Chile carved huge images into the dry earth or made images with layers of stone and dirt. These images are called geoglyphs. The largest of these, the Atacama Giant, is a picture of a god measuring 282 feet (86 m) from head to toe.

Araucanians traveling through the mountains of Chile.

By 1450, a great empire had developed in the Peruvian Andes. The Inca Empire controlled lands that extended into areas that are now Colombia, Bolivia, Argentina, and Ecuador. In 1461, Inca forces entered Chile and won control of lands as far south as Santiago. Beyond this point, various Araucanian groups united to fight off the Inca. In the years that followed, the Araucanians traded with the Inca and learned some of their skills, such as weaving.

The Indigenous Peoples of Central Chile

When the Spanish arrived in Chile, they called all the people they met in the central and southern regions Araucanos, or "Southern People." The English version is Araucanians. Those people belonged to many different groups. The Picunche lived along the Maule River in what is now central Chile, while the Huilliche lived farther south, closer to the modern city of Valdivia. The Pehuenche lived west of the Andes, and the Puelche lived east of the mountains. The Mapuche lived farther south. Together, the groups were often called the Mapuche, a name still used for the major indigenous group of Chile.

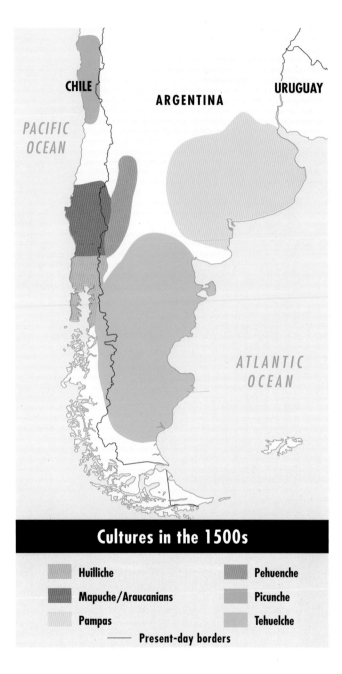

Cultures in the 1500s

- Huilliche
- Mapuche/Araucanians
- Pampas
- Pehuenche
- Picunche
- Tehuelche
- —— Present-day borders

CHILE · ARGENTINA · URUGUAY · PACIFIC OCEAN · ATLANTIC OCEAN

Starting in the 1400s, the kingdoms of Spain and Portugal sent out ships to explore distant lands. England, France, and other countries soon joined them. In 1520, Portuguese explorer Ferdinand Magellan was seeking a westward sea route from Europe to Asia. He and his crew found a waterway that separated the southern tip of mainland South America from Tierra del Fuego. This waterway is now called the Strait of Magellan.

Magellan and his crew did not stop in Chile. Instead, they sailed on across the Pacific. The next European to reach Chile was a Spaniard named Diego de Almagro. He was a conquistador, a soldier who helped Spain conquer the great empires of North and South America. Almagro fought the Inca in 1532, and three years later, he headed south from Peru to Chile in search of gold. After struggling through the mountains, Almagro and his men saw rich farmlands, but not the huge gold mines they sought, so they returned to Peru.

In 1540, Pedro de Valdivia led another expedition from Peru into Chile. He took a land route along the ocean and then headed up the Mapocho River. Along the way, he forced the local people to give him food and to work for him. Valdivia finally stopped at a spot he called Santiago, which became Spain's first permanent settlement in Chile. The men built adobe (mud-brick) homes covered with grass roofs. The local people disliked the way the Spanish had treated them before, so they attacked the village. The Spanish rebuilt Santiago and put it under heavier guard. Valdivia became governor of the settlement, which was under the control of Spanish leaders based in Peru. They, in turn, took orders from the Spanish king.

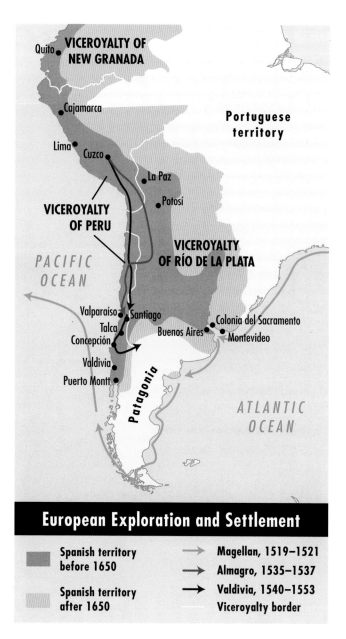

Growth and Conflict

Valdivia made the Mapuche work in the nearby gold mines. The labor system was called the *encomienda*. A Spanish master had control over all the people on his lands and could force them to work in mines or on farms. Unlike

African Conquistador

Pedro de Valdivia's army included an enslaved African named Juan Valiente. He convinced his owner to let him become a soldier, and Valiente fought well in both Guatemala and Chile. As a reward, he received land in Chile, along with indigenous workers. He was the first African in South America to win such an honor. Valiente later tried to buy his freedom from his owner. He gave an officer money to give to the owner, but the soldier ran off with it. Valiente died in 1553 battling the Mapuche.

Rebel Leader

A Mapuche named Lautaro, born around 1534, was forced to work as Pedro de Valdivia's servant. In that position, he learned about the Spanish methods of war and how to ride horses, which the Spanish had brought with them to Chile. Lautaro later escaped, and he began teaching other Mapuche how to ride and fight like the Spanish. He became the leader of a 1553 rebellion. Lautaro was killed in 1557 before he could lead a final attack on Santiago, but he is still honored as a symbol of Chilean pride and freedom.

slave owners, who could treat their slaves as property, the encomienda masters were supposed to treat the indigenous people well and teach them Christianity. But most masters treated the Mapuche harshly, though by law the indigenous people still owned their own land.

Valdivia soon started a new settlement to the north. South of Santiago, the Spanish founded the town of Concepción in 1550, and then the town of Valdivia shortly after that. The Spanish built their settlements close to the water so they could easily travel by boat to other parts of South America. At times, the Spanish moved large numbers of Mapuche from their homes to help the settlers raise crops.

By 1553, the Mapuche and others joined together and defeated the Spanish at the Battle of Tucapel. Valdivia died during the fighting. The Mapuche then marched north to Santiago, but the Spanish successfully defended their town.

After their loss to the Mapuche, the Spanish focused on their settlements in the central region rather than venturing too deeply into southern Mapuche lands. They also expanded eastward across the Andes into land that is now Argentina.

Early Economy and Society

Many indigenous people living near the Spanish died from European diseases for which they had no immunities. The Spanish bought enslaved Africans to add to the workforce, but their numbers were small compared with those in other South American colonies. After 1608, any indigenous Chilean who rebelled could be enslaved.

Chilean society, like Spanish society, had very distinct classes. The wealthiest and most powerful class was composed of people born in Spain. Below them were the *criollos*—Spanish people born in Chile. Next came mestizos, people of a mixed Spanish and indigenous background. Below them were enslaved people.

Sir Francis Drake was both a pirate and an explorer. He was the first Englishman to sail around the world.

The Colonial Centuries

By the beginning of the 17th century, about 10,000 Spanish settlers lived in Chile. Because of disease and war, the indigenous population had fallen from about 1 million to 500,000. Most of those who survived were Mapuche living in the south. The Chilean colony, unlike other Spanish lands in South America, had a permanent army. This reflected Spain's fears about the Mapuche and possible invasion by the Dutch and the English. Pirates such as Sir Francis Drake were also a threat. In 1577, Drake raided several Chilean towns.

Through the 17th century, most Spanish settlers worked in farming. On large farms called haciendas, indigenous and Spanish workers raised cattle and grain for the landowners. Most of the colony's leaders and other wealthy people lived in Santiago. Because Santiago was so far from government officials in Peru and Spain, the colony's leaders had a good deal of freedom.

Still, Spain tried to control life in its distant colony. The Spanish officials said that foreigners could not settle there, and all imported goods had to be transported through Panama. This control let Spain collect taxes on the goods. Chilean merchants sometimes broke the law and smuggled goods or traded with foreign merchants.

Later in the century, more Chileans played a role in running the colony. One of these local officials, Ambrosio O'Higgins, had come to Chile from Ireland. O'Higgins became governor of Chile in 1788 and tried to improve the local mining industry. He also ended the encomienda system and promoted business.

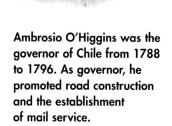

Ambrosio O'Higgins was the governor of Chile from 1788 to 1796. As governor, he promoted road construction and the establishment of mail service.

The Road to Independence

Changes in Spain brought changes to Chile. In 1808, Napoléon Bonaparte of France invaded Spain. He later removed the Spanish king and named his own brother Spain's new leader. In Chile, the most powerful criollos remained loyal to the old king. They decided to rule the colony themselves until the old king regained his throne and declared the country an independent republic with the Spanish monarchy on September 18, 1810. Some Chileans, however, saw the trouble in Spain

Revolutionary Sister

José Miguel Carrera and his brothers had an aide in their struggle for Chilean independence—their sister Javiera. She attended meetings when the rebels were first planning to take power. Later, she hid soldiers in her house, which also served as a drop-off point for weapons for rebels. Javiera is also said to have designed the first flag for an independent Chile. After people loyal to the Spanish king regained power in Chile, Javiera fled to Argentina, where she aided the rebel effort to take back the government.

Hero of Independence

Bernardo O'Higgins (1778–1842) was the son of an Irish father and a Chilean mother. For a time, his father, Ambrosio O'Higgins, was the leader of the Viceroyalty of Peru, which included Chile. The elder O'Higgins tried to improve conditions in Chile, but Bernardo thought that independence from Spain was the best way to improve life in Chile. In 1817, he commanded the army that defeated forces loyal to Spain. Bernardo O'Higgins was named Chile's supreme director, a position similar to president. He then set out to help other Spanish colonies in the region win their freedom. Today, O'Higgins is considered Chile's national hero, and many public places are named for him.

as their chance to win complete independence. José Miguel Carrera and his brothers took control of the government in 1811. They ruled briefly before Spanish troops and Chileans still loyal to the king rose against them. Carrera and Bernardo O'Higgins, Ambrosio's son, led the rebel forces. In 1814, the Spanish side defeated the rebels.

Before the Spanish regained control, the rebels had made reforms such as ending slavery and promoting trade without government restrictions. The rebels also created an elected government. The Spanish ended these reforms, which prompted more Chileans to support complete independence from Spain. Some joined with Argentine troops who wanted to force the Spanish from South America. In 1817, Bernardo O'Higgins led an army into Chile and defeated the troops loyal to Spain. This victory ensured Chile's independence, which was officially declared the next year.

José Miguel Carrera was one of the leaders of the Chilean independence movement. He served as commander in chief of the army in 1813 and 1814.

Ruling an independent Chile was not easy. The powerful people in the nation were divided. Church leaders and the wealthy did not want to make major changes from the past. They were called conservatives. Other Chileans wanted the people to elect their leaders and curb the traditional power of the church and wealthy criollos. They were called liberals. In the 1820s, a number of different governments ruled Chile, and liberals and conservatives fought a brief civil war.

Finally, in 1830, Diego Portales emerged as Chile's new leader, and he imposed order on the country. He called for a new constitution, which gave conservative landowners great power in Chile. Under this constitution, the president picked the men who ran for Congress. These men usually did as the president wanted. Only men who owned a certain amount of property could vote.

During this period, Chile's economy grew. Copper and silver mining became a major industry, and the city of

Copper and silver mining have long been important to the Chilean economy. This image from the 1820s shows Chileans at a copper and silver works.

Valparaíso served as an important trading center, with ships from all over the world entering its harbor. Immigrants from Germany and other countries started to settle in the south. Many farmworkers left haciendas to look for jobs in the growing towns, and the government built several thousand schools.

Railroads were built to many major Chilean cities, including Valparaíso, by the end of the 19th century.

By 1851, Chile had built the first railway system in South America, and a telegraph line soon followed. British and U.S. investors helped pay for some of these improvements, helping Chile become the most modern nation on the continent.

Wealth and order, however, were not enough for some Chileans. They wanted a greater say in their government. In 1851, a civil war broke out as liberals attacked the conservative government. Several thousand people died in the fighting. President Manuel Montt ended the rebellion with help from Great Britain. Montt was the last powerful conservative president of the era, as liberals slowly gained power in the government. In 1874, liberals gave the voting right to all adult males, ending the requirement that voters own property. Radicals, people who sought even greater change and more power for people who were not elite, also emerged to challenge the liberals and the conservatives.

PERU

Lake Titicaca

Tacna

Arica

Pisagua

Iquique

Pozo Almonte

Calama

Antofagasta

Taltal

Miraflores

Copiapó

La Serena

BOLIVIA

Lake Poopó

PACIFIC OCEAN

CHILE

ARGENTINA

War of the Pacific

Chile in 1879

gained from Bolivia, 1884

gained from Peru, 1884

gained from Peru, 1884; awarded to Chile, 1929

gained from Peru, 1884; awarded to Peru, 1929

Present-day border

In the mid-1800s, Chile sometimes battled its neighbors. During the 1830s, Peru and Bolivia briefly united. Chile already had trade disagreements with Peru, and it feared the united power of the two countries. Chile declared war on the new union in 1836. Chile's troops won a major victory in 1839 and forced the two countries to separate.

In the 1860s, relations between Chile and Bolivia became tense as the two argued over their border in the Atacama Desert. Then, in 1879, fighting broke out over mining rights and taxes in the region. Peru came to Bolivia's aid during this conflict, called the War of the Pacific. Chile had a smaller army than its two enemies, but in 1883, it won the war and took land from both Bolivia and Peru.

During this time, the Chilean government also battled the Mapuche. Since the 16th century, the Mapuche had lived independent of the Spanish and then the Chilean government. In the mid-19th century, however, Chilean settlers and soldiers slowly pushed south into Mapuche lands. In

1881, the Mapuche attacked the forts and towns around them, but the Chilean military was stronger and defeated them. The Chileans took over most Mapuche lands, and the Mapuche began a long struggle to receive fair treatment.

In 1891, another civil war erupted in Chile, over the power of the president. The existing government opposed efforts to give Congress more power in the running of the country. But the rebels, who supported giving more power to Congress, won the war.

Challenges in a New Century

Chile's victory in the War of the Pacific had given the country a new source of money. The lands it gained had valuable nitrate mines. Nitrate was used in fertilizer and gunpowder, and Chile sold its nitrate around the world. The mines in the north attracted workers from all over the country. So did the growing cities of Santiago, Valparaíso, Concepción, and Valdivia, where factories made clothing, food, and other goods.

The mine and factory workers toiled in dangerous jobs for low wages. They wanted a better life. By the early 1900s, miners began to form unions, groups that would fight for higher pay and better working conditions.

Mapuche leaders gather for a portrait in the late 19th century.

Bloody Times

To win their demands for better pay, union members sometimes refused to work, in an action called a strike. In 1907, miners went on strike in Iquique, in northern Chile. The government sent in troops, who shot and killed miners and their families. At least 500 people were killed or wounded. Violence sometimes broke out during later strikes, but the attack on the Iquique miners was the worst ever in Chile.

Soon, however, the economy faced new problems. Companies began producing artificial nitrate. Chile's nitrate mines began to close, putting miners out of work.

Miners, factory workers, and the middle class—office workers, clerks, owners of small businesses—wanted an even larger role in Chilean government. In 1920, they helped elect Arturo Alessandri president. Alessandri tried to make changes to help the workers and the middle class, but conservatives opposed him. He did manage to draw up a new constitution, which balanced powers more equally between the president and Congress.

By the end of the 1920s, the military began to play a large role in Chilean politics. Officers supported candidates or at times took over the government. Alessandri returned as president in 1932, when Chile was suffering the effects of the worldwide economic downturn known as the Great Depression. During this time, mines and factories closed and thousands of Chileans lost their jobs.

Arturo Alessandri was president of Chile from 1920 to 1925 and from 1932 to 1938.

During the early 20th century, many farmers moved into Chile's southern regions. Here, oxcarts make their way through a remote town.

Postwar Growth

World War II (1939–1945) helped pull the world out of the Depression as countries spent money to build their militaries. Chile did not get involved in the war, but it was developing close ties to the United States. That relationship upset some Chilean radicals, who favored socialism, an economic system in which the government owns most factories. Other radicals supported communism, which supports government ownership of business and calls for a single political party to control the government. Most Chilean leaders had long favored private ownership of most businesses. U.S. companies bought some important Chilean companies, especially in copper mining. Socialists and communists opposed the growing American influence in their country. People with different political views—conservative, liberal, and radical—competed for control of the government.

Meanwhile, more Chileans became members of the middle class, and the Sur became a leading farming region. Starting in the 1930s, newcomers had cleared forests to raise cattle and grain. New laws let more people vote—including women—and voters took a strong interest in the parties and their plans for Chile. In the early 1960s, the government began land reform. It paid the owners of large haciendas for unused land and gave it to peasants.

Salvador Allende became active in politics while in medical school. He eventually served as the minister of health, as a member of the Chamber of Deputies, and as a senator before being elected president.

In 1964, a new party, the Christian Democrats, came to power. The goal of the Christian Democrats was to make sure all Chileans had food, housing, education, and legal rights. They took steps to improve education, building several thousand new schools. They also bought and ran copper mines and several other businesses that had been private.

Crisis in Government

During the 1960s, Chile was one of few South American countries that was not run by the military. It had a healthy democratic system. Voters could choose their leaders from a number of different political parties. In 1970, Chileans made history when they elected Salvador Allende the first socialist president in Latin America.

As president, Allende made many changes. He raised wages for workers and limited the price of some goods. But Allende made many enemies. The new government took over more farmland, angering the former owners. Conservatives who supported private ownership opposed his policies, as did some Christian Democrats. Some radicals also disliked Allende, thinking he should limit democracy and create a communist society.

Conflicts among the different groups within Chile led the military to take action. On September 11, 1973, military officers told Allende that they were seizing power. The officers had the support of the United States, which disliked Allende's socialist policies.

The Chilean officers offered Allende a plane to leave the country. Allende refused, so the air force bombed the president's home, and Allende died during the fighting. A group of top officers, called a junta, took over the government, and Chile entered its darkest period since winning its freedom from Spain.

For months, the military government arrested thousands of people they thought might threaten order in Chile. Soldiers tortured and killed some of them. The bodies of many of

Chile saw much political protest during Allende's time in office. Here, protestors block a street in Santiago in 1972.

the people who died were never found. They are called "the disappeared." Even people who left Chile were not safe. The government worked with foreigners to kill some Chileans who fled the country.

General Augusto Pinochet led the junta, and he ruled Chile through the 1980s. During military rule, the government burned books it disliked, limited the actions of labor unions, and controlled the media. Many Chileans opposed his limits on their freedoms, but others welcomed the order he brought to the country. The economy also strengthened for a time, as Chile stressed more private ownership of business. But the changes did not provide jobs for all Chileans who wanted them, and many people remained poor. The country faced even tougher times during the early 1980s, when the economy weakened.

A Hated Dictator

Augusto Pinochet (1915–2006) said he ruled by force to keep order in Chile. His victims, though, saw him as an enemy of Chile's democratic government. Although he left the presidency in 1990, he made himself a lifetime member of the Senate, part of Chile's Congress. He also kept control of the military until 1998. Later that year, while in Great Britain, Pinochet was arrested for killing Spanish citizens during his first months in power. Instead of going to court in Spain, he was returned to Chile. The Chilean government also wanted to try him for past murders. Pinochet died while still fighting legal battles to avoid going to court.

Today and Tomorrow

In 1988, Chileans had the chance to decide if Pinochet would remain their president for eight more years. The voters said no, and in 1989, the country held its first free elections since 1973. Voters chose a Christian Democrat, and several socialist presidents followed. The country had successfully restored its democracy. Still, it remained haunted by the hard years under Pinochet. Many people had relatives who had been murdered by Pinochet's government, and people had lost their freedoms.

After many years of political oppression, Chile is again a free and peaceful country.

By the 1990s, Santiago and other cities had modern skyscrapers and pockets of great wealth. But in parts of the cities and in the countryside, about 40 percent of the people still lived in poverty. The presidents who followed Pinochet tried to use economic growth to help reduce poverty. Medical care and housing have improved, especially since 2000. The government has restored legal rights to unions and others who lost them under Pinochet. Women have also taken a more prominent role in government. In 2006, Michelle Bachelet was elected Chile's first female president.

Chileans face many challenges ahead as they try to solve their country's problems. The Chilean tradition of hard work and respect for order should help them meet those challenges.

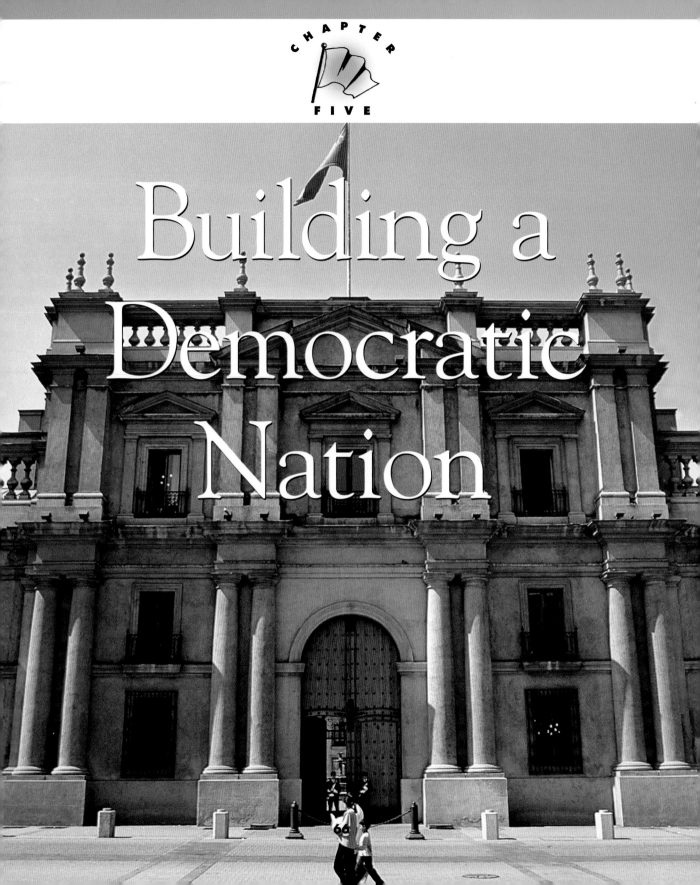

CHAPTER FIVE

Building a Democratic Nation

CHILE IS A REPUBLIC, A COUNTRY IN WHICH THE people control the government. Through its history, Chile has sometimes struggled to build a true democracy, one in which every adult has a say in making laws. The dictatorship of Augusto Pinochet ended a long period of democratic rule. Since he left power in 1990, Chileans have worked to restore freedom and democracy.

Chile's basic laws and system of government are outlined in its constitution. The country has had several constitutions since it first declared its independence in 1810. The current constitution was written in 1980 and has been amended, or changed, several times. Chile's constitution outlines three distinct parts of government, called branches: the executive, the legislative, and the judicial.

Opposite: **The presidential palace in Santiago houses the offices of the president and other top government officials.**

The Flag of Chile

Chile's flag has a broad red stripe across the bottom. The red symbolizes the blood shed during the fight for independence. Above the red stripe is a stripe of white, which stands for the snow on the Andes. In the upper left corner is a square of blue, representing the sky. A white star symbolizing honor and pride appears in the blue square. The flag was adopted in 1817.

The National Anthem

Eusebio Lillo Robles wrote the words to the Chilean national anthem, and Ramón Carnicer y Battle wrote the music.

Spanish Lyrics	English Translation
Puro, Chile, es tu cielo azulado;	Pure, Chile, is your blue sky;
Puras brisas te cruzan también.	Pure breezes flow across you as well.
Y tu campo de flores bordado	And your flower-embroidered field
Es la copia feliz del Edén.	Is a happy copy of Eden.
Majestuosa es la blanca montaña	Majestic is the white snow-capped mountain
Que te dio por baluarte el Señor	That was given you as a bastion by the Lord
Que te dio por baluarte el Señor,	That was given you as a bastion by the Lord,
Y ese mar que tranquilo te baña	And the sea that quietly washes your shores
Te promete futuro esplendor	Promises you future splendor
Y ese mar que tranquilo te baña	And the sea that quietly washes your shores
Te promete futuro esplendor.	Promises you future splendor.
Dulce Patria, recibe los votos	Sweet fatherland, accept the vows
Con que Chile en tus aras juró:	That were given by Chile at your altars:
Que o la tumba serás de los libres	Either you be the tomb of the free
O el asilo contra la opresión	Or the refuge against oppression
Que o la tumba serás de los libres	Either you be the tomb of the free
O el asilo contra la opresión	Or the refuge against oppression
Que o la tumba serás de los libres	Either you be the tomb of the free
O el asilo contra la opresión	Or the refuge against oppression
O el asilo contra la opresión	Or the refuge against oppression
O el asilo contra la opresión.	Or the refuge against oppression.

The Executive Branch

The executive branch carries out the laws of a country. The leader of Chile's executive branch is the president, who is elected every four years. If more than two candidates run and none of them receives more than half the vote, the top two vote-getters face each other in a special election. A president cannot serve two terms in a row, but he or she can leave office and run again after four years.

Chile's president proposes laws, offers amendments to the constitution, and appoints certain government officials. These include regional governors and cabinet members, who lead specific executive departments and advise the president on important issues. Executive-branch departments include National Defense, Finance, Foreign Affairs, Justice, Environment, and Health.

With the Senate's approval, Chile's president also appoints the comptroller general, who examines how money is collected

Ricardo Lagos served as president of Chile from 2000 to 2006, before four-year terms were in place.

Madame President

In 2006, Chileans elected their first female president, Michelle Bachelet. She became active in politics while she was in medical school during the presidency of Salvador Allende. Like Allende, Bachelet is a socialist. Her father, an air force general, served in the Allende government. He was arrested when General Pinochet took power and later died in prison. Michelle Bachelet was also arrested and briefly held in prison. After her release, she lived overseas until 1979, when she returned to Chile and completed her medical degree. After Pinochet left power, she served as Chile's minister of health and then minister of defense. As president, Bachelet has focused on improving Chile's schools and medical system and limiting corruption.

Building a Democratic Nation **69**

and spent at the national and local levels, making sure all laws are followed. The comptroller general also examines presidential orders, called decrees, and new laws to see if they follow existing laws and the country's constitution. A president can overrule a comptroller general's decision against a decree, but every cabinet minister must approve the president's action.

The Legislative Branch

The legislative branch proposes laws for Chile. Chile's legislature is called the National Congress, and it meets in Valparaíso, though most other government activities take place in the capital, Santiago. The National Congress has two

President Bachelet speaks to the National Congress. The Congress meets in Valparaíso, 85 miles (140 km) west of Santiago.

NATIONAL GOVERNMENT OF CHILE

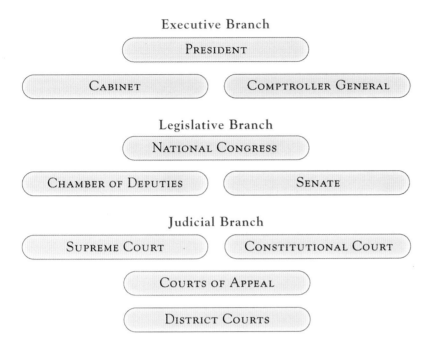

Executive Branch

PRESIDENT

CABINET   COMPTROLLER GENERAL

Legislative Branch

NATIONAL CONGRESS

CHAMBER OF DEPUTIES   SENATE

Judicial Branch

SUPREME COURT   CONSTITUTIONAL COURT

COURTS OF APPEAL

DISTRICT COURTS

parts, the Chamber of Deputies and the Senate. The Chamber of Deputies has 120 members, and the Senate has 38 members. Deputies serve for four years, while senators serve for eight. Once Chileans turn 18, they can vote in elections.

Members of the National Congress have other duties besides proposing laws. Both the deputies and the senators must approve international treaties before they take effect. The Chamber of Deputies can investigate if the president or other officials have broken the law. If they have, the Senate acts as a jury to decide whether they are innocent or guilty. The Senate must also approve certain officials appointed by the president, including some judges.

Members of the Chilean Supreme Court preside over a case. The court has 21 members, but smaller groups of at least 5 try each case.

The Judicial Branch

The judicial branch hears court cases involving law enforcement and disputes between groups or people. Chile's judicial branch has more than 500 courts. At the lower levels of the system are district courts that focus on certain areas of law such as crimes, family issues, disputes between workers and their employers, and crimes committed by teens. Above these courts are 16 courts of appeal, where justices decide if cases tried at the lower level were fair and followed the law. Cases heard in the courts of appeal can themselves be appealed to Chile's highest court, the Supreme Court, which meets at the Courts of Justice in Santiago. The president appoints the Supreme Court's 21 members for life. They must be approved by the Senate.

Chile also has a separate Constitutional Court that decides if laws follow the country's constitution. Special courts hear cases involving members of the military, and an elections court makes sure that all elections are carried out fairly.

A Changing Legal System

Until recently, Chile's legal system was based on one used in Spain and France during the 19th century. In criminal cases, judges investigated the facts and then reached a verdict.

The new legal system in Chile is more like the system used in the United States. A lawyer called a prosecutor works for the government and brings charges against an accused person. The accused person hires a defense lawyer, or the government appoints one if the defendant cannot afford one. This defense lawyer and the prosecutor present their evidence in court. It is up to the prosecutor to present enough evidence to show that the accused is guilty. The judges decide if the accused is guilty and then determine the punishment.

Regional and Local Governments

Chile is divided into 15 different regions, which are in turn divided into provinces. The president appoints the governors of the regions and the provinces. Unlike states in the United States, regions and provinces in Chile do not have their own legislative branches.

Elected mayors govern towns and cities. Local councils are supposed to offer advice to the mayors on social and economic issues. These councils, however, are new, and are not in place in every town.

Joaquín Lavín was the mayor of Santiago from 2000 to 2004.

Santiago: Did You Know This?

Santiago, Chile's capital and largest city, was founded in 1541. A few buildings date back to the colonial era, while modern skyscrapers rise above some streets. Santiago's city center sits 1,700 feet (520 m) above sea level, while nearby mountains in the Andes reach almost 18,000 feet (5,500 m). Average daily temperatures are a comfortable 75°F (24°C) in January and 47°F (8°C) in July.

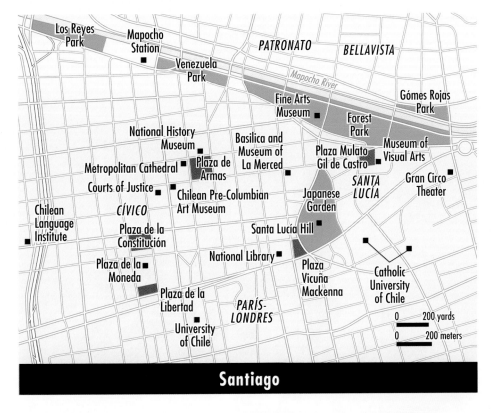

Santiago

Santiago has a population of about 6 million. Residents of the capital city live in 32 distinct neighborhoods. Some are marked by expensive buildings, while others have sprawling markets where handmade goods from across the country are sold. A popular gathering spot is the Plaza de Armas (left), the heart of the city since its founding. Several important buildings line the plaza, including the National History Museum (right) and the Metropolitan Cathedral. A little farther away, an old railway station, Mapocho Station, now serves as an art and convention center. Santiago is also home to several fine parks and gardens. Forest Park, which runs along the Mapocho River, is home to Chile's finest art museum, the National Museum of Fine Arts.

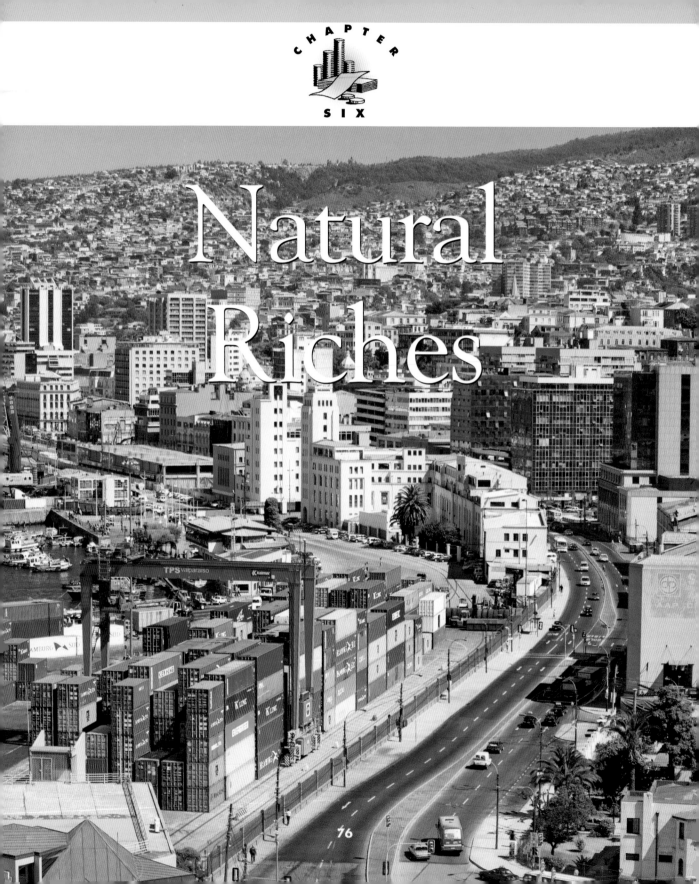

Natural Riches

I N COLONIAL DAYS, SPAIN TRIED TO LIMIT TRADE BETWEEN Chile and the world. Today, Chile's economy is built around international trade. Chile has signed many free-trade agreements with other countries, which allow goods to be bought and sold without restrictions or import taxes. These trade agreements helped Chile export goods worth almost US$59 billion in 2006. That figure is almost four times the amount exported a decade earlier. The goods sold abroad reflect the wide range of natural resources found in Chile, as well as the hard work of the Chilean people who turn resources into finished goods.

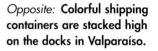

Opposite: **Colorful shipping containers are stacked high on the docks in Valparaíso.**

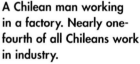

A Chilean man working in a factory. Nearly one-fourth of all Chileans work in industry.

Natural Riches **77**

Riches from the Earth

Mining copper and other ores has long been Chile's major industry. These minerals made up more than 60 percent of Chile's exports in 2007. Chile has the world's largest known reserves of copper, and in 2008, a new reserve was found. This discovery means that Chile will continue to be the world's most important source of copper for years to come. CODELCO, the government-owned copper company, produced 2 million tons (1.8 million metric tons) of copper in 2004.

Chile is also a world leader in mining molybdenum, an ore that is mixed with other metals to make them stronger. Other mines produce iron ore, gold, sodium and potassium nitrate, zinc, silver, and coal.

A power shovel scoops rock and dirt into a truck at La Escondida, the largest copper mine in the world.

Forests and Farms

Trees cover more than 32 million acres (13 million hectares) of land in Chile. Growing the trees, cutting them, and processing them provide jobs for more than 150,000 Chileans. Forest products are Chile's second-leading export, after copper. Radiata pine and eucalyptus trees are especially important to the industry,

which is centered on the southern coast. The trees are turned into lumber, cardboard, paper, and wood products such as door frames.

Logging plays a major role in the Chilean economy. Logs are Chile's second most valuable export, trailing only copper.

"Chicago Boys" in Chile

The Mattes have long been one of the richest families in Chile. Their wealth was built on timber, but Eliodoro Matte has expanded into new areas, including shipping and financial services. Matte and his closest relatives are Chile's only billionaires. During the early 1970s, Matte studied at the University of Chicago, where he and other Chileans learned economic ideas they put into place when they returned home. Matte and the others became known as the Chicago Boys, and their push to promote local businesses and free trade helped Chile's economy grow.

What Chile Grows, Makes, and Mines

Agriculture (in acreage planted, 2004)

Table grapes	120,000 acres (49,000 ha)
Apples	89,190 acres (36,095 ha)
Avocados	59,303 acres (24,000 ha)

Manufacturing (export value, 2007)

Processed foods	$6.04 billion
Chemical products	$3.01 billion
Cellulose and paper products	$2.92 billion

Mining (total production, 2006)

Copper	4.9 million metric tons
Iron ore	4.5 million metric tons
Sodium nitrate	0.9 million metric tons

Workers load peaches onto a truck in Chile. In 2005, Chile exported nearly $100 million worth of peaches.

Many crops grow well in Chile's rich soil. When it is summer in Chile, it's winter in North America, Japan, and Europe. Chilean farmers export many fruits and vegetables to these areas when it's too cold to grow them in the Northern Hemisphere. Chile produces more grapes than any other country in the world, and it is the second-leading producer of avocados. Other top crops include apples, plums, peaches, and berries. Vegetables grown in Chile for export include onions, garlic, and asparagus. Most wheat and other grains are consumed in Chile, not exported.

Chileans don't just grow food for the world—they process it, too. Chile's grapes are used to make wine and raisins, its tomatoes are turned into tomato paste, and berries and other items are frozen or canned for later use. Chileans also process milk and other dairy products and turn livestock into meat.

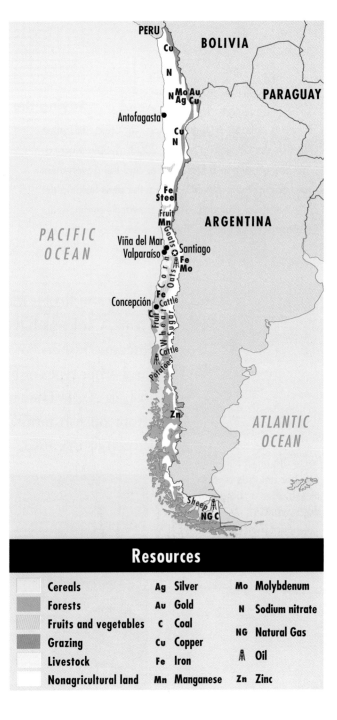

Resources

Cereals	Ag Silver	Mo Molybdenum
Forests	Au Gold	N Sodium nitrate
Fruits and vegetables	C Coal	NG Natural Gas
Grazing	Cu Copper	Oil
Livestock	Fe Iron	Zn Zinc
Nonagricultural land	Mn Manganese	

Fishing for Food

Off Chile's Pacific coast, the Peru Current carries cold water northward from Antarctica. This current helps create perfect

Saving the Salmon

Farming salmon is big business in Chile, so when the fish started getting sick in 2008, people worried. Millions of salmon began to die, and the government said part of the problem was that the pens holding the fish were too crowded. These crowded conditions let disease spread quickly. The fish were also getting too much of a medicine that was supposed to keep them healthy. The bacteria that cause disease were evolving, changing over time so they were better able to resist the drug designed to kill them. To keep the salmon healthy, Chile made plans to lower the number of salmon in each pen and reduce the use of certain drugs.

living conditions for a wide variety of fish. Over the last thirty years, Chileans have made fishing one of their top sources of income. Fishers catch sea bass, shellfish, anchovies, mackerel, and other types of fish. Chileans caught 5 million tons of wild fish in 2004. They also raise a growing number of salmon and trout on fish farms. Most of this fish is sent overseas, either frozen or in cans.

A fisher unloads crates of fish after a successful day's work.

A worker makes sun-dried adobe bricks near Talca in central Chile.

Manufacturing

Compared with mining, fishing, and agriculture, manufacturing plays a fairly small role in Chile's export economy. But in 2007, manufacturing created 17 percent of Chile's gross domestic product—the total of all the goods and services produced within the country. Factories near the main cities of central Chile make a variety of goods used within Chile, and a few that are sent abroad. These include textiles, plastic and paper packaging, and machinery. Much of the machinery is used to process goods from Chile's mining, forestry, and farming industries. Chileans also make iron, steel, and cement. Many of these products are used in the local construction industry.

Producing energy for Chileans is one key industry. In the Bío-Bío region of central Chile, oil is refined for use as gasoline. Some oil is turned into chemicals. The country's rivers also help supply energy. In hydroelectric plants, rushing water turns large blades called turbines to produce energy.

More than 60 percent of Chilean workers are employed in service industries such as sales.

At Your Service

About 63 percent of Chileans work in the service sector of the economy, which includes a wide range of businesses. Government services, education, retail sales, banking, insurance, health and legal services, communications, and tourism are all are part of Chile's service economy.

Because Chile has a well-educated workforce and laws that promote business, it has become a financial center for

Studying the Skies

A few Chileans provide a service peering into outer space. La Silla, in the Atacama Desert, is the site of 18 large telescopes. The site was chosen because it offers clear views of the skies, and telescopes work best when they are far from city lights.

Chilean Money

Chile's basic unit of currency is the peso. Chile issues coins worth 1, 5, 10, 50, 100, and 500 pesos and bills worth 1,000, 5,000, 10,000, and 20,000 pesos. Chilean bills depict prominent Chileans. For example, the 10,000-peso bill shows Captain Arturo Prat, a hero of the 1879–1883 War of the Pacific. Prat commanded a wooden ship that was rammed by a metal one. Before his ship sank, Prat jumped onto the enemy ship to keep fighting. Though he was killed in the battle, his courage inspired other Chileans. In December 2008, US$1 was equal to 667 Chilean pesos.

South America. In 2004, the government and many businesses mapped out a plan to increase the use of computers and related equipment in Chile. This "digital agenda" aims to give more Chileans access to the Internet. Chile already leads South America in providing Internet access.

Many tourists travel to Chile to enjoy its beautiful scenery.

Tourism is also important to Chile's economy. Chileans and visitors alike enjoy sports such as kayaking and skiing, and a growing number of people are visiting Chile on cruise ships. In 2007, about 200,000 Chileans worked in the tourist industry at restaurants, hotels, and other places.

A Cultural Mix

H UNDREDS OF YEARS AGO, THE SPANISH ENTERED A land where many different indigenous groups lived. Many Chileans still trace their roots to Spain, yet hundreds of thousands of indigenous people still speak their own languages. Through the centuries, many indigenous people and Spanish people married and had children. Today, many Chileans are mestizos, people of mixed European and indigenous background. And since colonial days, immigrants have come to Chile from around the world, adding new elements to the country's customs and culture.

Opposite: **About 24 percent of Chileans are under age 15.**

Spain in Chile

Walking through Santiago and other Chilean cities, it's hard to miss the influence Spain had on this nation. The Spanish brought their language, their religion, and their customs

Who Lives in Chile?

Whites and mestizos	95.4 %
Mapuche	4 %
Other indigenous peoples	0.6 %

Speaking Spanish in Chile

Here are some vowels and consonants as they are pronounced in Chilean Spanish:

Letter	Pronounce As	Example	Pronunciation
a	ah (as in father)	*azul* (blue)	ah-ZOOL
e	eh (as in set)	*once* (eleven)	ON-seh
i	ee (as in feet)	*diga* (speak)	DEE-gah
j	h (as in hat)	*naranja* (orange)	nah-RAHN-hah
ll	y (as in "yet")	*llave* (key)	YAH-veh
ñ	n and y (as in "yet")	*mañana* (tomorrow)	mah-NYAH-nah
qu	k (as in keen)	*quince* (fifteen)	KEEN-seh

Chilean children wave to passersby.

to Chile. Yet a Spaniard traveling in Chile today will hear people speaking unfamiliar Spanish phrases. Far distant from Spain, Chileans changed the Spanish language.

Speaking Spanish Like a Chilean

Chileans have some expressions not used in other Spanish-speaking lands. These are sometimes called *chilenismos*. Here are a few:

Chilenismo	Literal Meaning	Actual Meaning
al tiro	upon shooting	right away
¿cachai?	catch?	get it?/understand?
dejar la escoba	to leave the broom	to create a mess or disaster
monitos	little monkeys	cartoons

The Spanish who settled Chile came from various regions of Spain. A large number came from the Basque Country, a region along the Pyrenees Mountains between Spain and France. Basque merchants traveled with Pedro de Valdivia when he first reached Chile, and for many years, they made up almost half of all immigrants to Chile. Many Basques did well in business, and today many members of Chile's wealthiest families trace their roots to the Basque Country. More Basques came to Chile during the 1930s. A civil war in Spain forced many of them to flee, and Chile offered a welcoming new home.

In recent years, new Spanish-speaking people have immigrated to Chile from neighboring countries such as Peru, Bolivia, and Argentina. Chile's strong economy offers many of them jobs that they cannot find in their homelands. In 2002, some 48,000 Chileans had been born in Argentina, more than in any other country.

Persons per square mile	Persons per square kilometer
more than 259	more than 100
25–259	10–100
11–24	5–9
3–10	1–4
fewer than 3	fewer than 1

Population of Chile's Largest Cities (2006 est.)

Santiago	6,607,000
Puente Alto	627,263
Antofagasta	341,942
Viña del Mar	292,203
Valparaíso	276,474
Concepción	225,158

A woman wears an elaborate headdress during a festival in San Pedro.

Immigrants from All Over

During the early 19th century, Chilean officials sought newcomers from Europe, particularly Great Britain and France. The immigrants, it was hoped, would bring skills and money to help Chile grow. Later in the century, Chile recruited Germans to live in the Lake District. Some of these newcomers founded the town of Puerto Montt, and many of them opened businesses in Valdivia. German names are still common in these areas. Contemporary German Chileans still cook some of the meats and cakes their ancestors ate. Around the time the Germans came, small numbers of Italians, Swiss, and Slavs arrived as well.

Chile is home to an estimated 400,000 people of Palestinian descent. Palestinians began moving from the Middle East to Chile in the early 20th century.

Troubles in foreign lands often drove some people to seek freedom and jobs in Chile. Starting in the early 20th century, Arabic-speaking people from the Middle East began to arrive. Most came from Lebanon and Syria. Many of them settled in the town of La Calera, in the Valle Central. The descendants of these and other Arab settlers still live in Chile.

Chile has a small Asian population that includes Koreans, Chinese, and Japanese. Most of the Japanese came to Chile after first settling in other parts of South America.

What's in a Name?

Chileans often have two surnames. The first of the two family names comes from the father's family, and the second comes from the mother's. Often, however, only the father's last name is used. The full name of Chile's first woman president is Michelle Bachelet Jeria, but she is usually called simply Michelle Bachelet. Like most Chilean women, she kept her own name when she married.

A Mapuche boy blowing a musical instrument called a *trutruca* marches through Santiago.

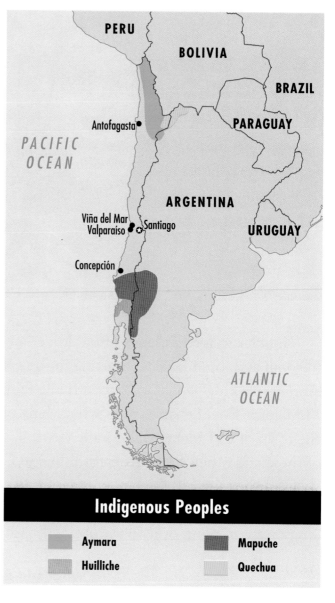

PERU

BOLIVIA

BRAZIL

PARAGUAY

PACIFIC
OCEAN

Antofagasta

ARGENTINA

URUGUAY

Viña del Mar
Valparaíso ● Santiago

Concepción

ATLANTIC
OCEAN

Indigenous Peoples

Aymara   Mapuche

Huilliche   Quechua

Indigenous Peoples

Chile has a little more than 1 million indigenous residents. The largest single group is the Mapuche. Just over half the country's 900,000 or so Mapuche live in and around Santiago. Others live in the traditional lands in the south. A Chilean law gives indigenous peoples the right to live according to their ancient customs and protects the boundaries of their lands. Still, the indigenous peoples of Chile face many problems. In general, they make less money than white or mestizo Chileans, and they face prejudice when trying to find jobs and housing.

Mapuche means "People of the Earth," and the Mapuche fought hard to resist Chilean control of their lands. In some villages today, the Mapuche are demanding their former lands, and the government has sent in troops to stop their protests.

The next-largest indigenous group is the Aymara, with a population of about 90,000. Most Aymara live in the northern Andes and the altiplano, near the borders of Bolivia and Peru. Many Aymara have moved to cities along the coast, although about 30,000 still farm and raise cattle. They live near the Quechua, another Andean people. Only a few thousand

Speaking Like a Mapuche

The Mapuche language is called Mapudungun. It has six vowel sounds:

a as in "man"

e as in "end"

i as in "pin"

o as in "cold"

u as the *oo* in "moon"

the sixth vowel, *ï*, sounds like an English *u* but with the lips placed as if saying "e."

Here are some words in Mapudungun:

kiñe (one)

epu (two)

kíla (three)

nuke (mother)

chaw (father)

Some Mapuche words are used throughout Chile. The name for the national flower, copihue, is a Mapuche word, and so are the names of many geographic sites.

Keeping Languages Alive

In recent decades, the number of Chileans who speak the country's indigenous languages has fallen. Many indigenous people have taught their children Spanish as they moved into the cities looking for jobs. Starting in 2008, the Chilean government began promoting the teaching of the Mapuche language, called Mapudungun, and other native languages, even among nonindigenous children. The first of several day care centers opened to teach children of all backgrounds simple words in Mapudungun and the languages of the Aymara and Rapa Nui. The goal is to help the children, especially those from nonindigenous families, learn more about the customs and lives of Chile's indigenous people.

Opposite: **The moai statues are the symbols of Easter Island.**

Quechua live in Chile today. Another indigenous group in the north is the Atacameños. They mostly farm, using canals to carry water across the dry desert region.

The indigenous people of Easter Island are the Rapa Nui. Today, only a few thousand Rapa Nui remain, and most are mestizos. The Rapa Nui try to preserve their old ways while welcoming tourists who come to see the large stone sculptures that dot the island. Called moai, these sculptures stand about 20 feet (6 m) tall and depict human heads with large foreheads and pointed chins. The Rapa Nui carved them between 1250 and 1500 CE.

African Chileans

A small number of Chileans trace their roots to Africa. The Spanish did not bring many enslaved Africans to colonial Chile. They did bring Africans to Arica, Peru, however, and that region became part of Chile after the War of the Pacific ended in 1883. Arica remains a center for African Chilean culture.

Spiritual Life

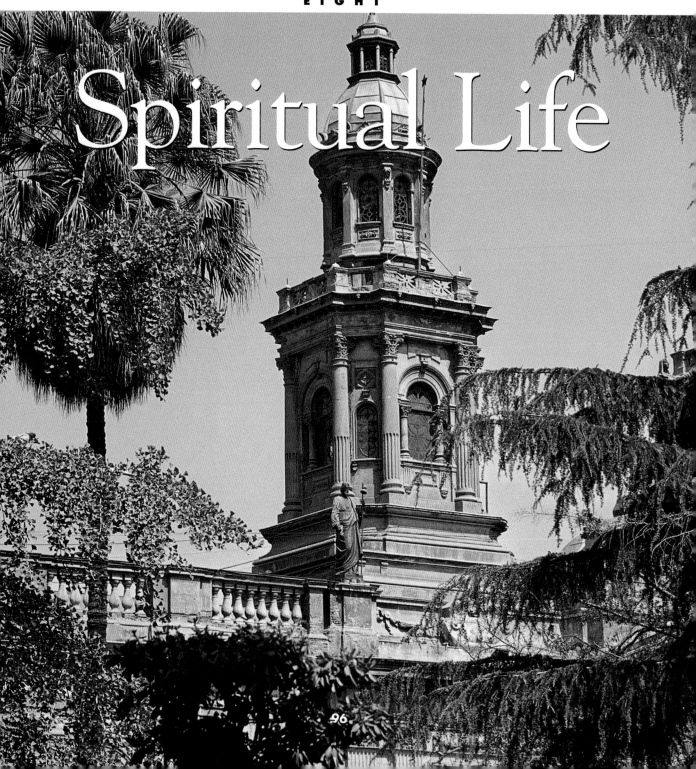

When Pedro de Valdivia led a Spanish expedition into Chile in 1540, he traveled with Roman Catholic priests. Spanish officials wanted to spread their country's Catholic faith in all its colonies. The priests tried to teach Roman Catholic beliefs to the indigenous peoples. Some Aymara and Mapuche converted, and others resisted. Many indigenous people blended their traditional beliefs with Catholicism.

Opposite: **Metropolitan Cathedral stands on the Plaza de Armas, in the heart of Santiago.**

A statue of Pedro de Valdivia

Religions of Chile (2002)

Roman Catholicism	70%
Evangelicalism (Protestant)	15.1%
Jehovah's Witness	1.1%
Other Christian religion	1%
Judaism, Islam, and other non-Christian religion	4.6%
None	8.3%

Over the centuries, immigrants from other lands brought new faiths to Chile. Today, the country is home to people who follow Judaism, Islam, Buddhism, and a variety of Protestant beliefs. By law, Chileans can worship as they choose, and the government does not restrict the actions of any church. The Roman Catholic Church, however, remains the largest and most powerful church in the nation.

Catholicism Yesterday and Today

In colonial days, all Spanish Chileans belonged to the Catholic Church, and priests worked closely with government officials to keep order. Some priests, however, opposed the colonial government's harsh treatment of Chile's indigenous peoples.

Women pray in a church in Chile in 1939. Roman Catholicism has been the dominant religion in the country since the Spanish first arrived in the region.

A Chilean Saint

A modern priest who left his mark on Chile was Alberto Hurtado Cruchaga. Padre Hurtado, as he was called, grew up poor in Chile in the early 20th century. As a priest, he dedicated himself to helping the country's less fortunate, especially children who had no parents or home. He raised money to build homes for the children and later added homes for poor men and women. The homes offered classes so that the residents could improve their lives. Hurtado also worked to improve the rights of Chile's workers, supporting the growth of labor unions. Hurtado died in 1952. In honor of his good works, the Roman Catholic Church named him a saint in 2005.

After Chile gained independence, some of its leaders tried to weaken the power of the Roman Catholic Church. The leaders did not want the church to influence the government. They did not want it to dictate laws or have sole control over marriage. Some Chileans resisted the effort to weaken the church's influence. The struggle between devout Catholics and citizens opposed to mixing government and religion continues. Divorce, for example, is against Catholic teachings, and Chile did not allow divorce until 2004.

Chile's Roman Catholics have at times been a conservative force, resisting change. But, as in colonial times, some recent Chilean church leaders have spoken out against social problems and inequality. During and after General Augusto Pinochet's rule, the church tried to help victims of government torture. In recent years, Chile's Catholic officials have supported the rights of the Mapuche.

Some people crawl during a pilgrimage to the Church of the Virgen de lo Vasquez in Valparaíso. One man is carrying a model of that same church. Hundreds of thousands of people make the pilgrimage each December.

The Catholic Church remains strong in Chile. It runs schools and colleges and has influence with business leaders. Children in Catholic families are baptized soon after they are born and are expected to go through other important Catholic rites. These include first communion, confirmation, and marriage in a Catholic church.

Chilean Catholics honor their church's saints and Mary, the mother of Jesus. Festivals and parades mark the days set aside for the saints. In July, the town of La Tirana holds a celebration for the Virgen del Carmen, also known as Our Lady of Mount Carmel. The lively festival features dancers in costumes and is one of the nation's most important religious festivals.

Other Christian Groups

Under Spanish rule, only Catholics could live in Chile. When Chile became independent, however, the new government welcomed Protestants who could help the economy grow.

Many English merchants who settled in Chile belonged to the Anglican Church. Most German settlers who came in the 19th century were Lutherans. Today, Chile's Protestants also include Methodists and Presbyterians. Most Protestants in the country are Pentecostal. In Pentecostal churches, the services are filled with emotion and music, and some members believe that their faith can cure the sick.

Other Christian churches in Chile today include Greek Orthodox and Armenian Orthodox. Chile also has a growing number of Mormons, who belong to the Church of Jesus Christ of Latter-day Saints, and Jehovah's Witnesses.

A large Mormon temple sits in Santiago. Chile is home to more than 540,000 Mormons, the fourth-largest Mormon population in the world.

Members of Santiago's Jewish community show their support for the Jewish nation of Israel.

Other Faiths

A few of the first Spanish settlers in Chile were Jewish. Over time, more Jewish people came to Chile from other parts of Europe and from Argentina. Some became prominent in government and business. Today, about 15,000 Jewish people live in Chile, mostly in Santiago and other major cities.

Chile has a small number of Muslims. The country's first mosque, for Muslim religious services, was built in 1990. Today, the country has three mosques and a Muslim population of about 3,000. Chile is also home to small Buddhist and Baha'i populations.

Mapuche Beliefs

About two-thirds of Chile's indigenous people belong to the Catholic Church. Still, many Mapuche hold on to their traditional beliefs. The Mapuche believe that the world is filled with positive and negative forces. Ngenechén is the god of the positive, such as love and life, while Wekufu is the god of death. The Mapuche believe that mounds they built long ago are living things filled with the spirits of the dead. Honoring and making contact with the dead is a large part of Mapuche faith. In some Mapuche lands, priests called *machi* still hold ceremonies at the mounds. They take people inside the mounds to feel the presence of the spirits.

Music is an important part of Mapuche tradition.

The machi also keep track of their people's history, heal the sick, and conduct rites. Machi are said to be able contact the spirits or gods through their dreams. Both men and women can be machi, and new machi learn their skills from older machi.

Island Chapels

When Spanish priests reached Chiloé in the 17th century, they converted many local residents to Christianity. Chiloé at this time was covered with forests, and the indigenous people there built small, wooden chapels. They did not have nails, so they used wooden pegs to hold the chapels together. The outside of the chapels reflected European architectural style, while inside, the local builders used their own artistic styles. By the late 1800s, the people of Chiloé had built about a hundred of these chapels. Today, they are recognized as a unique blend of indigenous and Spanish culture.

Chilean Creativity

A LOVE OF WRITING GOES BACK CENTURIES IN CHILE. Pablo Neruda, a great Chilean poet, said, "Chile has an extraordinary history . . . because [it} was invented by a poet." He was referring to Alonso de Ercilla, a 16th-century Spanish soldier who fought against the Mapuche. He was also a poet, and he wrote Chile's first great literary work, *La Araucana*. The poem describes the conflict between the Spanish and indigenous peoples. De Ercilla also saw the bravery of the Mapuche as they fought to preserve their way of life. Thanks to *La Araucana*, many future Chileans also came to admire the Mapuche.

Opposite: **Sofia Gandarias painted this portrait of Pablo Neruda, a great Chilean poet.**

Alonso de Ercilla published *La Araucana* in three parts, beginning in 1569.

Poets and Novelists

For many years, Chile's best-known writers were its historians and others who tried to make sense of the country's fight for independence and its growth. Then, in the 20th century, poetry took center stage. Across the country, writers formed poetry societies, where they could share their works with others. The first major 20th-century Chilean poet was Vicente Huidobro, who published his first poem in 1910 while still a teenager. Huidobro wanted to create a new kind of poetry that did not simply describe the world around the poet. Instead, he thought the poet should create something new out of his own mind.

In the 1920s, Gabriela Mistral published her first major book of poems in New York, though she had already published some of her work in Chile. Unlike Huidobro, Mistral wanted to describe things she saw and knew firsthand, including friendships, childhood, and motherhood. In 1945, she was awarded the Nobel Prize for Literature, the greatest prize for any writer. Mistral was the first Spanish-speaking poet, and the first Latin American woman, to receive the honor.

Mistral helped the career of the great Chilean poet Pablo Neruda. When Neruda was still a boy, Mistral showed him the works of other important poets. Neruda was influenced by them and by the mestizo culture of Chile and his experiences traveling in other countries. He often wrote about the struggles of everyday Chileans to improve their lives. In 1971, Neruda also won the Nobel Prize for Literature.

Chile has produced novelists, too. José Donoso began publishing novels during the 1950s and went on to become one of the greatest modern writers in

In addition to being a well-respected writer, Gabriela Mistral was also an important educator and diplomat in Chile.

South America. His work is sometimes called magical realism. It mixes seemingly impossible situations into the lives of regular people, often with plenty of humor. His major works include *The Obscene Bird of Night* and *The Garden Next Door*. Isabel Allende began writing novels during the 1980s, starting with *The House of the Spirits*. Allende, a niece of former Chilean president Salvador Allende, fled Chile after he was overthrown. Her book *My Invented Country* describes growing up in Chile and her lasting ties to her home-

Isabel Allende has written more than a dozen novels.

land. Roberto Bolaño was born in Santiago and spent many years living in Spain and Mexico. In 1973, he worked briefly with Chileans who were trying to resist the rule of General Augusto Pinochet. Bolaño died in 2003, and several years later, his major books began to appear in English. *The Savage Detectives*, in particular, won great praise.

Castaway

Robinson Crusoe is sometimes considered the first novel written in English, and many people know its story of a man stranded on a remote island. What many people do not know is that it was inspired by a real person's experiences in Chile. In 1704, Alexander Selkirk was sailing on a ship. He got in an argument with the captain and asked to be left on one of the Juan Fernández Islands, off the coast of Chile. No one lived on the island, and Selkirk survived by eating wild goats that the Spanish had earlier left on the island. Selkirk was finally rescued in 1709. English author Daniel Defoe used Selkirk's experiences in the Juan Fernández Islands as the basis for his character Crusoe. Today, the island where Selkirk lived is called Robinson Crusoe Island, and another nearby island is named for Selkirk.

The zampoña, or panpipe, is at the heart of Chilean music. Musicians play the instrument by blowing horizontally across the end of the pipe.

Music and Dance

The indigenous peoples of Chile play a variety of drums, pipes, and other instruments. The *zampoña*, a kind of panpipe, has a series of tubes with one end open and one closed. The tubes are various lengths and are tied together from shortest to longest. Blowing into the different-length tubes creates different notes. The *wada* is a dried pumpkin filled with seeds or stones. A musician shakes the wada, making the seeds rattle to create a rhythm.

When the Spanish arrived, they brought guitars with them. From guitars evolved a Chilean stringed instrument called the *charango*, which has five sets of two strings. The backs of the charango were once made from the shells of the quirquincho, a relative of the armadillo.

After the arrival of the Spanish, a popular type of traditional musician in Chile and neighboring countries was the *payador*, who traveled from town to town with a guitar, making up songs on the spot. Later, musicians sometimes formed clubs called *peñas*, where people gathered to play and hear folk music.

Starting in the 1960s, Chile's tradition of folk music inspired new singers and songwriters such as Violeta Parra and Victor Jara. They wrote songs that used familiar Chilean music but added words that described the struggles of Chile's poor and working class. This new folk music was called *nueva canción Chilena*, or "Chilean new song."

A Way with Words and Music

Violeta Parra was born to a poor but artistic family in 1917. At an early age, she sang in public to make money, and for a time, she and her sister performed as a duo in Santiago. While raising a family, she began to record songs that she wrote and played throughout Latin America and Europe. She also researched earlier Chilean folk music and helped a new generation learn about it. She is usually credited as the "mother" of *nueva canción Chilena*. Parra was also an artist, making sculptures and tapestries. In 1967, she wrote her most famous song, "Gracias a la Vida" ("Thanks to Life"). Her children Angel and Isabel Parra also sang folk music, and her grandson Angel helped form the rock group Los Tres, the first Chilean band to appear on MTV's *Unplugged*. Violeta Parra died in 1967.

Other musicians trace their musical roots to Chile's indigenous population. Illapu, a band that was influenced by the native music of the Andes, was popular in the 1970s and still plays today.

Dancing is important in Chilean culture. In central Chile, the *sombrerito*, or "little hat," is a popular dance. At one point, the dancers make a figure eight as they move around a hat placed on the ground. In a Mapuche dance called the *choiquepurun*, the dancers imitate the movements of the rhea, Chile's ostrichlike bird.

Indigenous people perform a dance in the streets of Santiago.

President Michelle Bachelet (in red) joins in dancing the cueca at an event in 2006 celebrating Chilean independence.

The *cueca* became the official dance of Chile in 1979. It's thought to have its roots in either West Africa or Europe. In it, men dress like cowboys and women wear colorful dresses. The cueca is said to copy the actions of a rooster trying to attract a hen. A man selects the woman he finds the prettiest, and the two hold onto a handkerchief. The man pulls on the cloth to bring the woman closer to him, and soon both dancers are stomping their feet. Bafona, a dance troupe that has performed all over the world, showcases many of Chile's folk-dancing traditions.

The National Museum of Fine Arts

Chile's major art museum is the National Museum of Fine Arts. Located in Santiago, the museum has a large glass dome that lets natural light stream into its main space. It sits in Forest Park, a large park with artwork scattered around it. The National Museum of Fine Arts features art from Chile and welcomes traveling shows by international artists. The building in which it is housed is also the site of the Museum of Contemporary Art, which displays the latest art from Chile and other parts of Latin America.

Chile has a strong tradition of mural painting. This one depicts the mining industry in the town of María Elena.

Visual Arts

Chile has produced a number of talented visual artists. Roberto Matta, who worked with many European artists during the 1920s and 1930s, was part of the surrealist movement, which explored dreams and the mind. In more recent years, Arturo Duclos has used both paint and objects such as human bones to create images. Gonzalo Cienfuegos often paints human figures in scenes from everyday life, though the scenes are more like comics than real life.

Chile also has a tradition of folk art. On many city streets, artists have painted murals—large, colorful paintings on buildings and walls. Pomaire, outside of Santiago, is home to many talented potters. Artists in Chile also make baskets and create carved items and jewelry out of lapis lazuli, a native blue stone.

Ariel Dorfman is a playwright, novelist, professor, and human rights activist.

On Stage and Screen

Santiago is the center of Chile's theater scene. During the summer, the popular Teatro a Mil, or "Theater for a Thousand" (meaning "a thousand pesos"), offers performances. Its low ticket prices give everyone the chance to see puppet theater, readings, operas, and plays. Ariel Dorfman, one of Chile's greatest playwrights, often writes about oppressive governments and the struggle for freedom. His play *Death and the Maiden* examined the torture that took place during the Pinochet years.

Since democracy returned to Chile, some Chileans have been making movies. *Machuca*, a 2004 film by Andrés Wood, is set in 1973 and deals with the concerns of a typical Chilean boy during one of his country's most violent years.

Entertainment That Helps

Each November, millions of Chileans gather around their TVs to watch *Teletón Chile*, a telethon to raise money for disabled children. During the telethon, entertainers perform and ask viewers to call in with donations. The telethon was started in 1977 by Don Francisco, the popular host of a TV variety show called *Sábado Gigante*, which is shown in many other countries. Francisco's real name is Mario Kreutzberger, and he is a native of Chile. The telethon is his way of helping the less fortunate in his homeland.

Life in a Vibrant Land

114

CHILEANS HAVE A DEEP LOVE FOR MANY THINGS, including family, festivals, and food. Though Chileans are sometimes considered reserved, they love to laugh with friends, though their jokes may show what Chilean novelist Isabel Allende has called "a twisted sense of humor." The jokes often make fun of Chileans and problems in their government.

Although tradition is important, many Chileans, especially the young, embrace new things. They adopt styles and technologies that come from North America and Europe. Chile is a dynamic blend of old and new. The people reflect that mix in their daily lives.

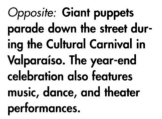

Opposite: **Giant puppets parade down the street during the Cultural Carnival in Valparaíso. The year-end celebration also features music, dance, and theater performances.**

Even while celebrating the traditions of their ancestors, Chileans enjoy the convenience of modern life such as cell phones.

There is no one kind of home life in Chile. In some areas of Santiago, families live in small shacks, while in other areas, rich people live in large homes, sometimes with guards outside gates. In the countryside, some Mapuche live in houses topped with straw roofs, just as their ancestors did centuries ago. The government has a program that helps young people buy their own homes. The houses are simple, and the residents are expected to add rooms on their own if they want more space.

Today, almost 90 percent of Chileans live in cities, with Santiago and nearby towns home to almost 40 percent of the country's total population. And conditions in Chilean homes are steadily improving. By 2002, 82 percent of families had a refrigerator, compared with only 55 percent ten years earlier.

Some Chileans live in traditional homes made of stone or adobe bricks with straw roofs.

Santiago has the largest subway system in South America. About 2.5 million people ride it every day.

A Day in the Life

For many Chileans, the day begins with a simple meal of buttered bread and coffee or tea. Then it's off to work. During the school year, parents often bring their children to classes, which start around 8:00 A.M. The parents then head off to work. Many people work past 6:00 P.M.

Chileans can get to work in many different ways. Santiago has a subway system, called the metro, as well as buses called *micros*. Buses run within and between most cities. A special kind of bus called a *colectivo* runs on a set route but will pick up and let off passengers wherever they want, like a taxi. In the countryside, people are more likely to use bikes and motorcycles to get around. In some remote areas, the roads are unpaved, and cars are rare.

On a typical day, the main meal comes at lunch and can last for several hours. Some businesses shut down during this time. In late afternoon, Chileans usually break for tea and snacks. They have their last meal of the day around 9:00 P.M. Many adults do not go to bed until midnight.

A Warm Welcome

When Chileans welcome guests, they typically shake hands and hug. Women and family members are greeted with a kiss. In more formal settings, a handshake is the usual greeting, especially for men.

The Role of Women

Women in Chile are less likely to work outside the home than women in other Latin American countries. Traditionally,

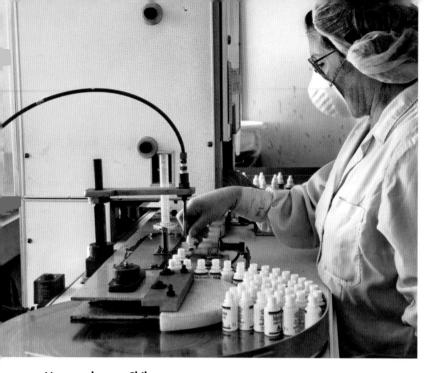

More and more Chilean women are entering the workforce. This woman works in the production of medicines.

Chilean women focused on their homes and children. Today, many families, not just the rich, have nannies or housekeepers to help take care of children and the house. These workers, almost always women, are often immigrants from neighboring countries.

One place where Chilean women have made gains is in the military. In 2001, the army and navy let women take military roles. Before this, women served only as support staff. The military also lets women train to be officers. By 2005, 20 percent of the soldiers training to be army officers were women. In 2007, the Chilean navy began allowing women to serve on ships.

Today, more Chilean women are going to college than ever before, and more work in professional fields, such as law and government. Education has played a large role in giving women these new chances.

Learning About Politics Firsthand

In 2006, some Chilean high school students took part in protests aimed at getting more government funding for education. Some of the rallies attracted hundreds of thousands of people. By the end of the year, President Michelle Bachelet had promised that the government would spend more money to help the neediest schools. She also agreed to put students on a panel that would discuss ways to improve education in Chile.

Education

Chileans believe strongly in the value of education. Almost 96 percent of the population can read and write. Children must start school at age 6 and remain in school until they are 14. About 80 percent of Chile's students complete high school. Along the way, they put in long hours. A recent study showed that the average school year in Chile lasts about 1,120 hours—longer than in any of the other industrialized nations studied.

Until grade 10, students throughout the country study the general academic subjects, which include reading, writing, math, science, and history. Beginning in grade 11, students can either stay focused on academic subjects or take classes that teach them skills related to specific jobs, such as manufacturing, forestry, or tourism.

About 15 percent of Chilean high school students attend private school.

The government offers free public education, but some children go to private school. In recent years, more of the best students from wealthier families have attended private school. The government has spent several hundred million dollars since the 1990s to give more public school students access to computers and the Internet.

The number of Chileans who continue their education after high school has risen greatly in recent decades. Only about 7 percent of students went to college in 1981, but by 2005, the number had risen to 37.5 percent. Students can go to four-year colleges and universities or to two-year schools that provide the skills needed to work as a technician in a particular field, such as agriculture.

Santiago is home to the country's oldest college, the University of Chile, which was founded in 1843. The capital is also home to the Catholic University of Chile. Other Catholic universities are located in Concepción, Temuco, and Valparaíso. Major non-Catholic schools are located in Atacama and Bío-Bío.

Some humitas are made with a mixture of corn and cheese. Others are made sweet or spicy using sugar or chili peppers.

Fine Food

To Chileans, fine food is an important part of life, and meals are a relaxing time filled with good talk. Meals usually include seafood or meat and a variety of vegetables. A common dish called *pastel de choclo* consists of meat, corn, eggs, and other ingredients baked together. To make a hearty stew called *cazuela*, potatoes, pumpkin, corn, peppers, rice, and meat are cooked together in a meat broth. *Ensalada chilena* is a common salad with tomatoes and onions. *Humita*, a

Marinated steak is on the menu at many Chilean asados.

dish with indigenous roots, is similar to a Mexican tamale. To make it, mashed corn is mixed with onion and basil and then wrapped inside corn husks. The stuffed husks are then baked or boiled. Humitas are a common fast-food meal.

A popular Chilean breakfast treat is *manjar*, made by setting an unopened can of sweetened condensed milk in boiling water for several hours. The cooking produces a thick, rich spread that can be smeared over bread. The heated, thickened milk is also used to make a dessert called *alfajor*. The manjar goes between layers of pastry dough, and the whole thing is covered with powdered sugar.

During warmer months, Chileans head outdoors for *asados*. Like barbecues in the United States, these meals feature meat roasted over hot coals or a fire. Steak or a roast is usually the main course. In Patagonia, whole goats or lambs are sometimes cooked over a fire, and diners carve off as large a piece as they want. Grilled meats are sometimes served with a sauce called *pebre*, which is made from tomatoes, onions, peppers, and spices.

A Soccer Star

Born in Santiago, soccer legend Iván Zamorano earned the nickname Bam Bam for his hard kicks, which helped him score almost 300 goals during his career. Zamorano played four seasons with Real Madrid, one of the top soccer teams in the world, and was a member of Chile's national team from 1987 to 2001. In 2004, FIFA, the international governing body of soccer, named him one of the top players ever. With his playing days over, Zamorano is trying to create a sports university in Chile to train teachers in physical education and coaching.

Leisure Time

Sharing a meal is just one way Chileans spend their free time. They also enjoy a wide range of sports. The most popular sport in Chile is soccer. Children and adults like enjoy playing the game and cheering on their local teams.

Basketball and tennis are also popular. Anita Lizana was one of Chile's early tennis stars. In 1937, she became the first South American woman to win one of the four Grand Slam

Still on Top

Many Chilean kids enjoy playing with a very old toy. They spin *trompos*, or tops, on sidewalks and streets. Most tops are made of wood with a metal rod in the center. Kids wrap string around the top and then quickly pull the string away, making the top spin. In one game, players draw a circle on the street and try to keep their tops in the circle. In another, players use their top to try to knock their opponents' tops out of the circle.

events, the top tournaments in tennis. During the 1970s, Hans Gildemeister was a top player, and in recent years, the hard-hitting Fernando González has been one of the game's leading players.

Tennis player Fernando González displays the silver medal he won at the 2008 Olympic Games.

A Chilean Vacation

For vacations, many Chileans head to the beach or go skiing in the Andes. Some also enjoy hiking in the mountains or through the glaciers of the south. In 2003, the government began building the Chilean Trail, a network of 5,000 miles (8,000 km) of trails that will cross meadows, forests, deserts, and lava fields. After a long hike, Chileans enjoy relaxing in one of the country's almost 300 hot springs. Water filled with minerals bubbles out of the ground, and sitting in the hot springs is said to cure a variety of health problems.

Chile's geography gives people plenty of chance to enjoy the outdoors. Chileans enjoy skiing and snowboarding in the Andes. They sail and swim in the Pacific Ocean and the country's many lakes. Surfing, windsurfing, rafting, and kayaking are also popular. One unusual sport in Chile is sandboarding. Dragon Hill, a large sand dune outside Iquique, is a hot spot for this sport, which is similar to snowboarding.

Rodeo was named Chile's national sport in 1962. Rancagua is the home of the National Rodeo Arena, where a championship rodeo is held each year. In a Chilean rodeo, two *huasos*, or cowboys, work as a team to try to pin a steer against the arena wall. Teams compete against each other and earn points for how well they meet their goal.

Sandboarding has become a popular sport in northern Chile.

A woman wears traditional clothing at an Independence Day celebration in Santa Cruz, in central Chile.

Holidays

In September, the whole country celebrates the *fiestas patrias*, or "national holidays." The 18th and 19th of the month mark Independence Day and Armed Forces Day. The celebration sometimes starts a few days before, with parades and dances. On Independence Day, people meet in parks to eat, talk, and dance the cueca. The next day, they honor the Chilean military with more parades—and more eating. The festivities may also include rodeos and games. Another big holiday is New Year's Day, which features huge fireworks displays in Santiago, Valparaíso, and other cities.

Christmas and Easter are the major religious holidays. On Christmas Eve, many people go to church at midnight and then

Major Holidays and Festivals

January 1	New Year's Day
March–April	Easter Week
May 1	Labor Day
May 21	Naval Battle of Iquique
May/June	Corpus Christi
June 29	San Pedro
August 15	Assumption
First Monday in September	Day of National Unity
September 18	Independence Day
September 19	Armed Forces Day
October 12	Columbus Day
November 1	All Saints' Day
December 8	Immaculate Conception
December 25	Christmas

go home to open presents. The next day is filled with food, usually an asado since the holiday comes during the Chilean summer. On the Sunday after Easter, Chileans celebrate the fiesta de Cuasimodo, a tradition that dates back to colonial times. During this festival, priests, huasos, and local officials in towns around Santiago visit people too old or sick to attend mass. Several thousand people join them as they make their rounds, and after, they celebrate with food and dancing.

Long ago, Cuasimodo participants rode on horseback, and the huasos traveled with the priests to protect them from rob-bers. Today, the visitors often travel on bikes and motorcycles, and the cowboys are not needed for protection. They are just part of the tradition. The Cuasimodo, like Chile itself, has become modern while still holding on to the best from its past.

Priests use a horse-drawn carriage to visit people during the fiesta de Cuasimodo.

Timeline

Chilean History

Chile declares itself an independent republic within the Spanish monarchy.	1810
Spanish and Loyalist forces defeat rebels who want independence.	1814
Bernardo O'Higgins leads Chileans to victory against Spanish forces.	1817
Chile officially declares independence.	1818
Civil war erupts between liberals and conservatives.	1851
Chile wins the War of the Pacific and gains land from Peru and Bolivia.	1883
Government troops kill hundreds of striking miners and their families in Iquique.	1907
Gabriela Mistral is the first Spanish-speaking poet to win the Nobel Prize for Literature.	1945
The largest recorded earthquake ever hits Valdivia.	1960
Salvador Allende is elected the first socialist president in Latin America.	1970
Military leaders force Allende from power; General Augusto Pinochet takes control of Chile.	1973
Chile has its first free political election since 1973.	1989
Michelle Bachelet becomes Chile's first female president.	2006
Chile begins teaching indigenous languages in schools.	2008

World History

1804	Haiti becomes independent following the only successful slave uprising in history.
1823	The United States announces the Monroe Doctrine.
1861–1865	American Civil War
1914–1918	World War I
1917	The Bolshevik Revolution brings communism to Russia.
1929	A worldwide economic depression sets in.
1939–1945	World War II
1950s–1960s	African colonies win independence from European nations.
1957–1975	Vietnam War
1989	The cold war ends as communism crumbles in Eastern Europe.
1994	South Africa abolishes apartheid.
2001	Terrorists attack the World Trade Center in New York City and the Pentagon in Arlington, Virginia.
2004	A tsunami in the Indian Ocean destroys coastlines in Africa, India, and Southeast Asia.
2008	The United States elects its first African American president.

Fast Facts

Official name: Republic of Chile

Capital: Santiago

Official language: Spanish

Santiago

CHILE

- Cities of more than 200,000 people
- ○ Other cities
- ◎ National capital
- ⁙ Archaeological site

0 — 400 miles
0 — 400 kilometers

PERU
BOLIVIA
BRAZIL
PARAGUAY
BRAZIL
ARGENTINA
URUGUAY

Lauca Nat'l Park
Arica
Iquique
Calama
Loa R.
Las Flamencos Nat'l Reserve
Antofagasta

Diego de Almagro
Copiapó
Humboldt Penguin Nat'l Reserve
Vallenar
La Serena
Coquimbo
Ovalle
Fray Jorge Nat'l Park
Illapel
La Calera
Viña del Mar
Valparaíso
Santiago
El Morado Nat'l Mon
San Bernardo
Puente Alto
Rancagua
Constitución
Talca
Maule R.
Talcahuano
Chillán
Concepción
Los Angeles
Cañete
Bío-Bío R.
Temuco
Villarrica
Valdivia
Calle-Calle R.
Osorno
Llanquihue Lake
Monte Verde
Puerto Montt
Chiloé Nat'l Park
Castro

PACIFIC OCEAN

Gulf of Corcovado
Las Guaitecas Nat'l Reserve
Coihaique
Laguna San Rafael Nat'l Park
General Carrera Lake
Baker R.
Bernardo O'Higgins Nat'l Park
Torres del Paine Nat'l Park
Puerto Natales
Strait of Magellan
Punta Arenas
Tierra del Fuego
Hernando de Magallanes Nat'l Park
Alberto de Agostini Nat'l Park

ATLANTIC OCEAN

Chile

Chile's flag

Paine Mountains

Official religion:	None
Founding date:	February 12, 1818
National anthem:	"Himno Nacional de Chile" ("National Anthem of Chile")
Type of government:	Republic
Chief of state:	President
Head of government:	President
Area:	292,260 square miles (756,950 sq km)
Greatest distance north and south:	2,654 miles (4,270 km)
Greatest distance east and west:	216 miles (348 km)
Bordering countries:	Peru to the north, Bolivia to the northeast, Argentina to the east
Highest elevation:	Ojos del Salado, 22,572 feet (6,880 m)
Lowest elevation:	Sea level, along the coast
Average high temperatures:	In Santiago, 82°F (28°C) in January, 58°F (14°C) in July
Average low temperatures:	In Santiago, 52°F (11°C) in January, 35°F (2°C) in July
Highest average annual precipitation:	About 200 inches (500 cm), at the Strait of Magellan
Lowest average annual precipitation:	0.03 inches (0.08 cm), at Arica

Moai statues

National population (2008 est.): 16,454,143

Population of largest cities (2006 est.):

Santiago	6,607,000
Puente Alto	627,263
Antofagasta	341,942
Viña del Mar	292,203
Valparaíso	276,474
Concepción	225,158

Landmarks:
- ▶ *Wooden chapels,* Chiloé
- ▶ *Valle de la Luna,* Atacama Desert
- ▶ *Funiculars,* Valparaíso
- ▶ *Forest Park,* Santiago
- ▶ *Moai statues,* Easter Island
- ▶ *National Rodeo Arena,* Rancagua

Economy: Chile is the world's leading producer of copper. It also mines iron ore, sodium nitrate, molybdenum, gold, and silver. Agriculture, forestry, and fishing are also key sectors of the economy. Chile grows more grapes than any other country and is a leader in raising avocados, trees for cellulose and paper products, and salmon. Despite the importance of mining, agriculture, and forestry, 63 percent of Chileans work in the service sector of the economy. This includes retail sales, banking, insurance, education, health care, government work, and tourism.

Currency: Chilean peso. In 2008, US$1 was equal to 667 Chilean pesos.

Weights and measures: Metric system

Literacy rate: 96%

Currency

Chilean children

Common Spanish words and phrases:

sí	yes
no	no
por favor	please
gracias	thank you
de nada	you're welcome
buenos días	good morning
adiós	good-bye
ayer	yesterday
hoy	today
mañana	tomorrow
¿Como está usted?	How are you?
muy bien	very well
¿Dónde está . . . ?	Where is . . . ?

Notable Chileans:

Salvador Allende *President*	(1908–1973)
Michelle Bachelet *President*	(1951–)
Lautaro *Mapuche leader*	(c. 1534–1557)
Gabriela Mistral *Poet*	(1889–1957)
Pablo Neruda *Poet*	(1904–1973)
Bernardo O'Higgins *General and president*	(1778–1842)
Violeta Parra *Singer and artist*	(1917–1967)
Augusto Pinochet *General and president*	(1915–2006)

Michelle Bachelet

To Find Out More

Books
Nonfiction

▶ Lourie, Peter. *Tierra del Fuego: A Journey to the End of the Earth.* Honesdale, Pa.: Boyds Mill Press, 2002.

▶ Ray, Deborah Kogan. *To Go Singing Through the World: The Childhood of Pablo Neruda.* New York: Farrar, Straus and Giroux, 2006.

▶ Somervill, Barbara. *The Land of the Andes.* Chanhassen, Minn.: Child's World, 2005.

▶ Underwood, Deborah. *The Easter Island Statues.* Detroit: KidHaven Press, 2005.

Fiction

▶ Barron, T. A. *The Day the Stones Walked: A Tale of Easter Island.* New York: Philomel Books, 2007.

▶ Hughes, Brenda. *Folk Tales from Chile.* New York: Hippocrene Books, 1999.

DVDs

▶ *Chile and Easter Island.* Escapi Media, 2004.

▶ *Eden at the End of the World.* National Geographic, 2008.

Web Sites

▶ **Chilean Cultural Heritage Site** www.nuestro.cl/eng/default.htm *The first Web site dedicated to Chile's cultural heritage, with articles and samples of Chilean music and art.*

▶ **Chilean Government**

www.chileangovernment.cl

For information about Chile's government, history, geography, and culture.

▶ **Guide to National Parks**

www.gochile.cl/eng/Guide/
ChileNationalParks/Chile-
National-Parks.asp

For details on the wildlife in Chile's major national parks and wildlife reserves and park photos, along with practical information for travelers.

▶ **Mapuche International Link**

www.mapuche-nation.org/english/
frontpage.htm

Details the ongoing struggle of the Mapuche of Chile and Argentina to regain their land and traditional way of life.

▶ **The Santiago Times**

www.santiagotimes.cl/santiagotimes

The Web site of Chile's major English-language newspaper, with links to sister papers and other useful sites.

Embassies

▶ **Embassy of Chile**

1732 Massachusetts Ave., NW
Washington, DC 20036
202-785-1746
www.chile-usa.org

▶ **Embassy of Chile in Canada**

50 O'Connor Street, Suite 1413
Ottawa, Ontario K1P 6L2
Canada
613-235-4402
www.chile.ca/en/

Index

Page numbers in *italics* indicate illustrations.

divorce and, 99
economy and, 100
education and, 100
government and, 98-99, 100
holidays, 126–127, *127*
immigrants and, 98
indigenous people, 97, 99,
    102–103, *103*
Islamic, 98, 102
Jehovah's Witnesses, 98, 101
Judaism, 98, 102, *102*
machi (Mapuche priests), 103
Mapuche people, 102–103
Metropolitan Cathedral, 96
Mormons, 101, *101*
Muslims, 102
Pentecostals, 101
Protestantism, 98, 100-101
Roman Catholicism, 12, 97,
    98–100, 98
saints, 99, 100
Spanish exploration and, 97, 103
Virgen del Carmen festival,
    100
reptilian life, 32, 35, 37, 38
Robinson Crusoe Island, 107
rodeo (national sport), 125
Roman Catholicism, 12, 97,
    98–100, 98

S
salmon farming, 82
sandboarding, 125, *125*
San Pedro, *90*
Santiago, 10, *10*, *13*, 22, 23, 29, 47,
    49, 50, 51, 52–53, 59, 63, 65, 66,
    70, 72, *73*, 74–75, *74*, *75*, 87,
    90, 92, 93, 96, *101*, 102, *102*,
    109, 110, 112, *112*, 113, 116,
    117, *117*, 120, 126, 127
Selkirk, Alexander, 107

Senate, 64, 69-70, 71, 72
service industry, 84–85, *84*
silver mining, 56, *56*
soccer, 122, *122*
sombrerito (dance), 110
sooty terns, 37, *37*
South American sea lions, *32*
Spanish exploration, 48, 49, 103
Spanish language, 12, 87-88, 94
Spanish settlers, 12, 13, 39, 46, 49,
    51, 52–53, 87–89, 102, 108
sports, *28*, 122–123, *122*, *123*, 124,
    124, 125, *125*
Strait of Magellan, 18, 25, 48
Supreme Court, 72, *72*
Sur region, 24, 61, 90

T
Talca, 83
taxes, 53, 58, 77
Teatro a Mil ("Theater for a
    Thousand"), 113
Teletón Chile fundraiser, 113
television, 109, 113
Temuco, 120
tennis, 122–123, *123*
theater, 113, *113*
Tierra del Fuego, 19, 25, 37, 48
timber industry, 22, 79, *79*
Torres del Paine National
    Park, *27*
tourism, 84, 85, *85*, 119
towns. *See also* cities.
    La Calera, 91
    La Tirana, 100
    María Elena, *112*
    Puerto Montt, 90
    Puerto Varas, 24
transportation, 24, 57, *57*, *61*,
    117, *117*
tricahue parrots, 38

trompos (tops), 123
trutruca (musical instrument), *92*

U
University of Chile, 120

V
Valdivia, 20, 24, 28, 47, 51, 59, 90
Valdivian Coastal Range, 40
Valdivia, Pedro de, 49, 50, 51, 89,
    97, *97*
Valiente, Juan, 50
Valle Central region, 22, 28, 36,
    38–39, *39*, 91
Valley of the Moon, 22, *22*
Valparaíso, *15*, 22, 23, *23*, 56--57, *57*,
    59, *70*, 76, 90, *114*, 120, 126
Viña del Mar, 23, *23*, 90
Viña del Mar International Song
    Festival, 23
Virgen del Carmen festival, 100

W
wada (musical instrument), 108
War of the Pacific, 58, *58*, 59, 85, 94
weaving, 10, 47
wildlife. *See* amphibian life; animal
    life; insect life; marine life; plant
    life; reptilian life.
women, 10, 15, 61, 65, 91, 98, 103,
    111, 117–118, *118*
Wood, Andrés, 113
World War II, 61

Z
Zamorano, Iván, 122, *122*
zampoña (musical instrument),
    108, *108*
Zona Austral region, 24–25, 28,
    41–42, 43

Meet the Author

M ICHAEL BURGAN has written more than 200 books for young people, including *Belgium* and *The United States of America* for the Enchantment of the World series. Burgan has a degree in history from the University of Connecticut. In his spare time, he enjoys writing plays, traveling, and listening to music.

In researching this book, Burgan started with travel guides and scholarly books. The histories ranged from general views of Chile's entire past to more specific topics, such as the 1973 coup by General Augusto Pinochet. Burgan also read Isabel Allende's story of her life in Chile, which gave him a more personal view of both historic events and daily activities.

Burgan next turned to Web sites, especially ones from the U.S. government, international organizations such as the United Nations, and the Chilean government. Chile's long and deep relationship with the United States means that plenty of Chilean Web sites include English translations.

Key sources for current events were the online versions of the *Santiago Times* and the *Patagonia Times*. "They're aimed largely at English speakers living in Chile," Burgan says, "but they're great for travelers and students, too." The Internet also helped him make contact with Chilean officials and a U.S. citizen studying in Chile. "She, in particular, gave me some insights I couldn't find anywhere else."

Photo Credits

age fotostock: 82 (Digital Vision), 108 (Christian Handl)

Alamy Images: 126 (Cephas Picture Library), 43 bottom (Javier Etcheverry), cover, 6 (Robert Harding Picture Library Ltd), 90 (imagebroker), 2 (Galen Rowell/ Mountain Light), 85 top, 132 bottom (Glyn Thomas), 124 (Simon Vine)

AP Images: 12 (Roberto Candia), 101 (Jesus Inostroza), 13, 91, 102, 111 (Santiago Llanquin), 107 (Eric Risberg)

Arco Digital Images/Hans Reinhard: 38 bottom

Ardea London, Ltd./Francois Gohier: 42

Aurora Photos/Bill Bachmann: 115

Bridgeman Art Library International Ltd., London/New York/Ken Welsh: 44 (Museo Arqueologico Gustavo Le Paige de Walque, Chile)

Corbis Images: 26 (Theo Allofs), 110 (Ivan Alvarado/epa), 45, 92 left (Ivan Alvarado/Reuters), 88, 133 top (Tony Arruza), 19, 132 top (Atlantide Phototravel), 73 (Carlos Barria/Reuters), 62, 63 (Bettmann), 100, 114 (Eliseo Fernandez/Reuters), 38 top (Michael & Patricia Fogden), 37 top (John Francis), 99 (Tony Gentile/Reuters), 37 bottom (Farrell Grehan), 125 (Franck Guiziou), 76, 97 (Jon Hicks), 25 (Bob Krist), 96 (Larry Lee Photography), 17, 131 bottom (Francesc Muntada), 78, 79 bottom (Reuters), 64 (Christine Spengler/Sygma), 103 bottom (Hubert Stadler), 98 (John Swope Collection), 28 (Henrik Trygg)

Everett Collection, Inc./Eye Ubiquitous/ Rex USA: 9

Getty Images: 8, 30 (Steve Allen), 112 bottom (Martin Bernetti), 85 bottom (Bridget Besaw), 27 (Steve Casimiro), 69 bottom, 133 bottom (Timothy A. Clary), 77, 84 top (Felipe Dupouy), 80 (David W. Hamilton), 70, 72 (David Lillo),

122 (Mauricio Lima), 41 right (Clive Nichols), 106 (Leo Rosenthal), 46 (Joel Sartore), 20 (Frank Scherschel), 23 left (Marco Simoni), 61 (Three Lions), 113 (Jeff Vespa), 14 (Jaime Villaseca)

Images & Stories/Hakan Oge: 29

Inmagine: 67, 131 top

Lonely Planet Images/Brent Winebrenner: 121

Magnum Photos/Sergio Larrain: 109

Mary Evans Picture Library: 55, 104 (AISA Media), 47

Minden Pictures: 36 (Luciano Candisani), 7 top, 34, 41 left (Tui De Roy), 39 (Gerry Ellis), 43 top (Kevin Schafer), 40 (Martin Withers/FLPA)

Nature Picture Library Ltd.: 33 (Hermann Brehm), 22 bottom, 32 (Pete Oxford)

North Wind Picture Archives: 52, 53

Peter Arnold Inc./Ron Giling: 117

Photolibrary: 120 (Foodanddrink Photos), 74, 130 left (Kordcom Kordcom)

Photri Inc.: 116 (Arps), 84 bottom (Richard Nowitz), 112 top (Brent Winebrenner)

Robertstock.com/Paul Souders: 35

Science Faction Images/Ed Darack: 21

South American Pictures: 22 top, 31 (Peter Francis), 127 (Robert Francis), 50, 59, 105 (Tony Morrison), 79 top, 118 (Chris Sharp)

Superstock, Inc./Photononstop: 7 bottom, 86

The Art Archive/Picture Desk/Neil Setchfield: 10

The Granger Collection, New York: 60 (ullstein bild), 54

The Image Works: 57 (Alinari Archives), 119 (Stuart Cohen), 24, 65 (Rob Crandall), 69 top (Francis Dean/Dean Pictures), 23 right (Macduff Everton), 15, 16, 66, 83, 103 top (David Frazier), 75 bottom (Richard Lucas), 123 (Professional Sport/TopFoto), 95 (Roger-Viollet), 56 (SSPL).

Maps by XNR Productions, Inc.